CONTENTS

GREAT PERSONAL LETTERS FOR BUSY PEOPLE

GREAT PERSONAL LETTERS FOR BUSY PEOPLE

300 READY-TO-USE LETTERS
FOR EVERY OCCASION

Dianna Booher

McGraw-Hill
New York   San Francisco   Washington, D.C.   Auckland   Bogotá
Caracas   Lisbon   London   Madrid   Mexico City   Milan
Montreal   New Delhi   San Juan   Singapore
Sydney   Tokyo   Toronto

Library of Congress Cataloging-in-Publicati on Data

Booher, Dianna Daniels.
    Great personal letters for busy people : 300 ready-to-use letters
for every occacion / Dianna Booher.
       p.   cm.
    ISBN 0-07-006656-6
    1. Letter writing. I. Title.
BJ2101.B66 1997
395.4—dc21   97-9027
                                         CIP

McGraw-Hill

A Division of The McGraw-Hill Companies

7 8 9 0 DOC/DOC 0 2

ISBN 0-07-006656-6

The sponsoring editor for this book was Betsy Brown, the editing supervisor was Penny Linskey, and the production supervisor was Claire B. Stanley. It was set in Fairfield by Terry Leaden of McGraw-Hill's Professional Book Group composition unit.

Printed and bound by R. R. Donnelley & Sons Company.

McGraw-Hill books are available at special quantity discounts to use as premiums and sales promotions, or for use in corporate training programs. For more information, please write to the Director of Special Sales, McGraw-Hill, Professional Publishing, Two Penn Plaza, New York, NY 10121-2298. Or contact your local bookstore.

This book is printed on recycled, acid-free paper containing a minimum of 50% recycled, de-inked fiber.

INVITATIONS   245

JOB REFERENCES AND INTRODUCTIONS   265

ACKNOWLEDGMENTS

Special thanks go to several people for their help with this manuscript:

Kirby Haltom of ModelOffice for his help in suggesting subjects and "letter situations." Kirby was instrumental in organizing topics for our software version of these letters.

Amy Quigley, president of ModelOffice, for "spurring" me on to complete this fourth package in our software productivity suite.

Heather MacKenzie, staff writer here at Booher Consultants, Inc, for her help in generating letter situations and her preparation of the final manuscript.

Betsy Brown, my editor at McGraw-Hill, for her attention to detail and focus on making this usable book for the current fast-paced lifestyles of readers.

GREAT PERSONAL LETTERS FOR BUSY PEOPLE

SO WHY WRITE WHEN I CAN PHONE?

Who's got time to write a letter or note these days? Why not just pick up the phone and call? Several reasons: speed and efficiency, impact, tact, and courtesy.

SPEED AND EFFICIENCY

Yes, writing a letter, an e-mail, or a note can be faster than making a phone call. Let me explain: How often do you dial someone at an organization and get a live person—the *right* live person—on the first try? More routinely, you receive a recorded message and a beep. Then the person returns your call and leaves you a message. Telephone tag can waste hours and days. It is not atypical that when conducting your personal business you may have to make three or four calls over a period of 3 to 10 days to resolve a matter.

Consider this scenario. Let's say you have a problem with your checking account. The bank fails to credit your account with a deposit, returns a check to someone marked "insufficient funds," and then charges you a $20 fee for the returned check. You could call the customer service department at the bank to discuss the problem—if you have 3 to 5 minutes to wade through the phone recordings and menus to get to the right person. Then suppose that person says she'll take care of it. But she doesn't.

You call a second time and get another person on the line, who'll "have to research it" and call you back. You get a call back 2 days later from the bank agent saying she has corrected the error. You ask if she'll notify the merchant involved to explain that the bounced check was the bank's error rather than yours. The agent doesn't know if the bank can do that. She'll "check on it" with her supervisor. She calls you back a couple of days later to say, yes, she'll write the merchant to restore your good name. So you finally have the problem corrected—4 phone calls, 20 minutes' talking time, and 6 days later.

And that's *if things go well*. The more likely scenario is that the bank rep asks you to bring in or mail a copy of the deposit slip for the deposit that you say you made but never got credited to your account. You'll have to write a letter when mailing the deposit slip, explaining again everything you told the bank rep over the phone. Or, worse, you'll have to go into the bank to explain it all again in person. And then that person you phone or talk to at the bank often asks for written documentation of the situation before action can be taken!

I repeat: It's often much faster and more efficient to write a letter (fax it if you're in a hurry) with all the details and supporting documentation, and let the reader do the walking and researching and conferring to take the action you want. Calling can become a long, drawn-out process of telephone tag and frustration.

IMPACT

A personal letter or note has greater impact on the recipient than a phone call. A message in black and white always looks more objective, factual, and firm. In other words, because writing is more formal than talking, your message takes on more importance and punch.

When do you need that increased impact in personal situations? Demanding that your landlord make repairs in your apartment. Insisting that the medical clinic has overcharged you. Telling the insurance company you expect a larger settlement for the damage to your car or house. Persuading the university to readmit you after you've withdrawn with failing grades and unexplained absences. Urging your congressional representative to vote no on the new tax bill. Asking a clergy member for a job reference. Hitting your relative for a loan. Breaking a relationship for good. Demanding that the auto mechanic treat you fairly. Soliciting money for a charity that must have funds to survive. Demanding that the manufacturer refund your money on a defective product.

A letter demands more attention and a more serious response than angry words in person or on the phone.

For the same reasons, personal letters to express *positive* sentiments sound more heartfelt and purposeful. How? Expressing appreciation to a teacher for his contribution to your life. Thanking a friend for encouragement or help during a difficulty. Expressing your love to a spouse, parents, friends, or other relatives.

Letters and notes have impact—both positive and negative. They have staying power.

TACT

Most people think better on their seat than on their feet. That is, if they can take a few moments to collect their thoughts in a sensitive situation, their words are less apt to hurt someone's feelings and are more prone to protect the sensitivities of all concerned.

When do you need such tactful wording? Declining to write a job reference for a friend's son, who you think is a jerk. Turning down a friend or relative who wants you to lend money. Reminding members of your social club that they still haven't paid you their share for the going-away gift. Telling your friend you're sorry about the divorce. Reminding your neighbor that she still hasn't paid for the damaged sofa. Declining an invitation to a boring event.

You can be more tactful when you have the time to linger over appropriate phrasing for touchy situations.

COURTESY

Have you noticed that fewer and fewer people follow the accepted norms of etiquette in business and social situations? It's as if our lives move at such a fast pace that we can't be bothered with "little things"—like accepting or declining a party invitation, thanking people for gifts, or responding to someone's congratulatory message. But the well-educated, cosmopolitan, cultured few do still incorporate courtesy into their lives. That's why they stand above the crowd as people with "class."

The more technical our world becomes, the more acute the need for the human touch: Building rapport with coworkers, community leaders, and friends demands that you pay attention to what's going on in their lives and respond in a socially acceptable way. Recognize achievements in their lives. Express appreciation for volunteer work. Wish them well on anniversaries and birthdays. Express gratitude for help and encouragement. Congratulate them on happy occasions such as birthdays and graduations. Express sorrow at their losses. In a high-tech world, the human touch through written words builds strong relationships.

So for all these reasons—speed and efficiency, impact, tact, and courtesy—personal letters and notes can:

- Solve problems with businesses and government organizations
- Build goodwill in the community
- Improve relationships with family and friends
- Handle sensitive issues with tact
- Solicit charitable contributions of time and money
- Add power to potentially threatening or dangerous situations
- Clarify actions in routine personal business transactions
- Strengthen positions on moral, social, and political issues that need attention

In short, when you have a problem or situation that needs action, these model letters, e-mail messages, and notes can help you express yourself with passion, power, and speed.

ANNOUNCEMENTS

An announcement implies immediacy. The first rule of thumb about announcing an event such as an engagement or a wedding, divorce, birth, graduation, or retirement is that *your* announcement reaches the reader before the news travels by other means. If your announcement is old news, it has arrived too late.

Then put yourself in the place of the reader: What key details would you want to know? Most likely the names, places, locations, and dates. After these details, you'll want to address specific concerns or issues that will likely flood the reader's mind. If it's an engagement, what's the time frame on the wedding? If it's a wedding, will you be moving to live elsewhere? Will you be changing jobs? Is the family thrilled? If it's a retirement, what is the effective date and what are your plans? Are you in good health? What do you plan to do with yourself between 9 and 5?

Friends and family also appreciate knowing how you feel about the event, occasion, or situation. Are you proud, sad, hopeful, excited, expectant, or happy about the future? Of course, you do want to be sensitive about special circumstances, such as announcing a divorce. You'll want to avoid saying things that might reflect negatively on others involved or might make you appear to be bitter, angry, or insensitive. Generally, prefer to save the juicy, specific details for personal conversations.

Finally, use a personal, warm tone. Your announcement takes the place of a glowing smile, warm handshake, or loving hug that you would deliver in person.

• BIRTH OF CHILD •

Example 1

Dear Kimberly and Clark,

If you could see my face now, you'd say it was beaming. We have a new baby boy, born Wednesday, January 13, at 10 p.m. Todd Daniel weighed in at 8 pounds; by all indications, he's happy so far with his station in life.

Jason and I are so thrilled that he's healthy and raring to get on with living. As you know, we have waited so long for this happy change in our lives that we couldn't wait to share the news with everyone. We feel very blessed.

Sincerely,

• BIRTH OF CHILD •

Example 2

Dear Washington and Alejandra,

Elliot and Julie Begouin are pleased to announce the birth of their second daughter, Jeannie Marie Begouin. Both mother and daughter are doing well. (Elliot seems a bit shaken, however.)

Julie and Jeannie are scheduled to be released from the hospital tomorrow morning. Please feel free to phone or stop in at any time thereafter.

Jeannie was born at 12:43 in the morning at St. Joseph's Hospital in Phoenix. She weighs 7 pounds, 6 ounces, and has a tuft of black hair right in the middle of her forehead. She looks just like her father.

We look forward to hearing from you soon.

Sincerely,

The Begouin Family

• ENGAGEMENT •

For those of you doubters who thought that after 5 years it was never going to happen: The question has been asked, and an affirmative answer given. David Feldman and I are thrilled to announce our engagement to be married.

We haven't yet set a date for the wedding, but are looking at the last week in April as the most workable option so far. We'll let you know as soon as we do.

David's parents, Paul and Stella Feldman, have planned an engagement party in our honor. Enclosed is your invitation.

We hope to see you there.

Sincerely,

• GRADUATION OF SON OR DAUGHTER •

Lydia and Damon Wilson are thrilled to announce the graduation of their son Marcus Alexander from Texas State University.

Commencement exercises will be held Saturday, May 14, at Stratton Coliseum on the TSU campus in San Madrid. The ceremony begins at 9 in the morning. Your formal invitation is enclosed.

To celebrate the beginning of his postgraduate life, we are planning a graduation party in his honor. It will be held at our house, at 7 on the evening of the commencement ceremony. A map to the party is enclosed.

Marcus will graduate cum laude with a bachelor of science in biochemistry. He plans to attend graduate school to continue his research in that field, but he will take a year off first to get some real-world experience in the workforce.

We look forward to seeing you on Graduation Day!

• WEDDING OF SON OR DAUGHTER •

Dear George,

We are extremely proud and happy to announce the upcoming wedding of our daughter, Ana Cecelia Ricardo, to Armando J. Elizondo. They'll be married August 6 at our ranch at Route 202, San Antonio, Texas. The ceremony will begin at 6:30 in the evening and a reception will immediately follow.

We have been anticipating this happy day since Ana was born 26 years ago. And now we can barely control our excitement, knowing that she and Armando will begin their new life together. We have already grown to love and appreciate Armando as one of the family.

We'd love to have you attend the wedding and reception to celebrate with us. Please let us know if you will be attending by returning the enclosed reply card.

Sincerest regards,

• RETIREMENT •

Dear Friends and Family,

I'm sure that you'll be surprised to learn that I have finally decided to take the proverbial engraved gold watch and retire. After having been with R&R Associates for 15 years, I'm ready to take some time for other, more personal pursuits.

I plan to take 2 weeks for a celebration vacation, August 29 through September 11. So effectively, my last day as a member of the workforce will be August 26.

My career as an editor with R&R has been a fulfilling experience for me. I now look forward to facing new (postcorporate) challenges in my life. An art class, for example, at the local junior college. A cruise to the Caribbean. More importantly, I hope to spend more time with my family, particularly my grandchildren. And perhaps a trip to Spain?

Best wishes,

• DIVORCE •

Dear Uncle Peter and Aunt Audrey,

I am truly sorry to have to inform you that Michael and I have come to the conclusion that divorce is our only viable option.

We are expecting a quick settlement and harbor no ill feelings toward each other. We hope that you will try to understand and accept our decision, because we could both use your support right now.

For the time being, I am staying at the house, while Michael has moved in with a friend of his, Joseph Harris. You can reach him at 555-5555.

Thank you for your prayers and good wishes as we adjust to our new separate lives.

Sincerely,

• CLASS REUNION •

Dear Class of 19—,

Ten years just flashed before our eyes, and it's now time for our 10-Year Class Reunion! It's hard to believe it has been so long since we sat in English class together. It seems like yesterday...well, on second thought, it seems like a lifetime ago.

I hope you'll be free to attend the gathering of old friends. The reunion will be held Saturday, May 30, in the Matisse Ballroom of the Carlisle Grand Hotel. It's scheduled to begin at 7 p.m. and go until 2 in the morning. (We'll see who still has that youthful spirit!)

Advance tickets are $35 for alumni and $40 for guests. At the door, all tickets will be $50.

Please indicate on the enclosed RSVP card whether you plan to attend, and check the appropriate box if you're enclosing a check to purchase tickets in advance. If you'd like to pay by credit card, call 555-5555.

See you at the reunion!

P.S. The reunion committee has been working in earnest to locate everyone. But if some people you know haven't received an invitation yet, be sure to tell them about it or notify us so we can send them their own invitation.

• MOVE TO NEW LOCATION •

Dear Family and Friends,

I've done it! I finally moved into my new home. It took my "movers," to whom I am eternally grateful, an entire Saturday, but the task is complete. The house is newly organized and swept, stuff put away, furniture rearranged for a third time, and at last it's all livable. I really enjoyed the experience, but am glad it's over!

New address: 3412 Cordial Lane, Remington, IL 23857
New phone number: (555) 555-5555

I'd like to have an open house in the near future, but haven't firmed up those plans yet. I'll be sure to keep you updated.

Regards,

P.S. Many thanks to my "movers"—Uncle Jerry, Uncle Bill, Uncle Joe, and Uncle Steve. You made a whole lot of work seem easier.

APOLOGIES

Have you ever tried to apologize to someone and realized that your apology made things worse? It happens. Apologies are difficult because you're already dealing with a negative situation; the other person hears you from a negative state of mind.

Your challenge with an apology, therefore, is to disarm the other person as quickly as possible. In other words, you need to acknowledge the error or insensitivity immediately and focus on making things right. The first words out of your mouth should acknowledge your inappropriate or insensitive action, behavior, words, or circumstance.

And be specific with your wording. Not: "Look, I apologize, ok?" Not: "I'm sorry that I made you angry." Not: "I couldn't help it; I'm sorry." Instead, use specific statements that let your reader know you accept full responsibility:

"I am so sorry that I failed to include you on the guest list."

"Can you ever forgive me for being so careless with your jewelry?"

"I don't know what I must have been thinking when I said such an insensitive thing."

"I regret very much the embarrassment I caused by showing up so late for the party."

"My actions were totally inappropriate and thoughtless."

"Would you please forgive me for giving your phone number to those people?"

"I'd very much like to apologize for taking your car without asking."

"Would you accept my apology for not phoning you personally about the situation and asking your preferences before making the final plans?"

"I owe you an apology for not responding to your invitation sooner."

"I offer my apology for neglecting to tell you I would not be in town over the weekend after I had promised to house-sit."

After you acknowledge your responsibility, make an empathetic statement to let your reader know you understand the damage, pain, or embarrassment caused. For example:

"You have every right to be upset with the way this was handled."

"I understand your feelings in this case."

"I know you must have been so disappointed."

If you try to minimize the situation or repercussions, the other person will feel compelled to repeat over and over what difficulties or pain you caused. If, on the other hand, your comments demonstrate that you understand the consequences, the reader will more likely forgive and forget. But do keep your tone consistent with the circumstances. Profuse apologies over minor issues sound patronizing. And flippant apologies over major issues sound unempathetic and insincere.

Above all, avoid statements that sound like excuses. Stand up straight and take your lumps!

"You are quite right."

"I was totally out of line."

"I should have been more careful in my investigation."

"I made far too many assumptions in this case."

"It was my responsibility to inform everyone concerned and I failed to do that."

Finally, offer to make things right, if possible, or demonstrate your intention to do so in the future.

• FOR MAKING EMBARRASSING REMARK •

Dear Ms. Coe,

I owe you an apology. I know how much I embarrassed you a few days ago with my impulsive statement at the conference. I should have been more aware of and sensitive to your feelings.

If you could, please forgive me. Sometimes a spontaneous comment will get away from me before I've had time to think about what I'm saying. It's not an excuse; it's just an explanation for my insensitivity. I am genuinely sorry for the thoughtless remark.

Sincerely,

• FOR BEHAVING INAPPROPRIATELY •

Dear Mr. Jampolis,

I wish to offer you my most sincere apology. My late arrival and surly attitude at the meeting were both uncalled for and unacceptable.

I allowed my emotions to dictate my actions, even though I am well aware that that is not the protocol for business interactions. Please accept my apology for my inappropriate behavior and know that it will never happen again.

Sincerely,

• FOR FRIEND BEHAVING INAPPROPRIATELY •

Dear Mr. Prabakharan:

I want to apologize for my friend's behavior at the cocktail party Thursday afternoon. He doesn't often drink alcohol and hadn't eaten lunch that day, but that's no excuse for his intoxicated condition.

We are both embarrassed about the incident, and hope that you can forgive his behavior.

Generally speaking, Jeff is a well-mannered and likable person. Unfortunately, he exercised poor judgment when he chose to drink the other day.

If there is anything that either of us can do to make amends, please let me know.

My sincerest apologies,

• FOR BOUNCING CHECK TO FRIEND OR RELATIVE •

Dear Uncle Marcel,

I am so embarrassed about the bad check that I gave you last week. Obviously, I had made an accounting error in my check register.

Enclosed is a new check for the $560, plus the $20 administrative fee that your bank charges for depositing a check that doesn't clear.

Don't be afraid to cash it. This one will clear!

Sincerely,

Monica

• FOR FAILING TO PROVIDE INFORMATION •

Dear Peyton,

How could I have been so careless as not to have told you about the new client's specifications for his audiences in San Francisco? I don't know how, but it completely slipped my mind.

I apologize for neglecting to supply you with that valuable information. Today, I mailed a letter of apology to the client as well, explaining that your failure to meet his expectations was entirely due to my error.

To ensure that we are now clear on the matter, his specifications for future demonstrations are as follows:

- Use no slides.
- Keep the lights on at all times.
- Be as informal as possible.

In the future, I will be more diligent about providing you with such preferences up front.

Sincerely,

• FOR DAMAGING NEIGHBOR'S PROPERTY •

Dear Bao and Mai,

I think you'll be interested to discover who the culprits are who knocked over and then flattened your mailbox this morning. I saw the whole event because I, myself, was one of them.

I am so sorry for the incident. Please know that I take full responsibility for the damage and will be happy to reimburse you for a new mailbox. If you'd prefer, I can take the damaged one, order a replacement myself, and deliver it to your door. Please phone me at 555-8434 (my work number) and let me know whether you'd prefer to get the replacement installed yourself or have me do it.

I was giving my son a driving lesson this morning. Apparently, I was not doing a very good job, because he managed to take out your mailbox in the course of the lesson. Next time, we'll have the driving lesson in an empty parking lot.

Again, I apologize for the trouble we've caused.

Sincerely,

• FOR MISSING BIRTHDAY •

Dear Aunt Claire,

Happy belated birthday!

It is now 17 days since the day, and I, being the punctual person that I am, am finally expressing my wish that you experience all the happiness you deserve in your sixty-second year.

I am truly sorry that I missed the day with the rest of the family. Mother tells me that you had a wonderful time, despite my absentmindedness about the event.

You are still so special to me. Have a wonderful year, and I'll be in touch again shortly.

Sincerely,

• FOR MISSING FRIENDS' ANNIVERSARY •

Dear Terrence and Toni,

Guess what we forgot! I hope your anniversary celebrations were very happy despite our absence. And even though I'm sure they were (happy), we'd still like to make it up to you.

How does dinner at Hedari's sound? Washington and I would love to treat you on Saturday evening, May 4. I know it's been one of your favorite restaurants for years, and we've been dying to try it.

If you don't already have plans, why don't you meet us at our place around 6:30? We'll have cocktails on the patio before we head for the restaurant.

If you can't make it, just let me know and we'll reschedule for another night. We're both still traveling, so please phone and leave your answer on the recorder. Looking forward to celebrating with you—even if belatedly.

Regards,

• FOR MISSING DINNER DATE •

Dear Rick,

It was totally inconsiderate of me to have missed our dinner date last evening. No doubt, you are furious with me.

Please accept my apology. I'd like to make it up to you. Would you please allow me to treat you to dinner at the same restaurant next week?

I didn't have a chance to give you the details on the phone, but I had to work late because of some computer billing errors that have been accumulating for a month without anyone's knowledge. I kept thinking I could break away at any minute, but, obviously, not so. My secretary and I were at the office until 9:20 trying to solve the problem.

Agree to meet me next week, and I promise that I'll show up this time. Forgiven?

Sincerely,

• FOR BEING UNABLE TO ATTEND FUNCTION •

Dear Dr. Blackeagle:

As reluctant as I am to have to tell you, I will be unable to attend the Scholarship Ball on Saturday, March 20.

Please accept my apologies and pass them along to the other Scholarship Committee members and to the ball coordinators.

I have been looking forward to the ball with anticipation for several months, but when the date was finally settled, I found myself in a quandary. I have a prior commitment that I just cannot break.

Please keep me posted on future committee functions. I would very much like to help with other upcoming events.

Sincerely,

• For Not Having Written •

Dear Huang,

I apologize for not having responded to you sooner. I know that the important plans you have been contemplating depend on my answers, and I'm truly sorry that I haven't been more helpful and responsive.

In your letter you mentioned that you were considering expanding your business into South Korea. In answer to your question, I would be happy to offer whatever advice I can with regard to customs procedures, government policies on foreign investments, market predictions, cultural barriers, and the like. My previous experiences dealing with South Korea have left me with such a wealth of knowledge on the subject that I hardly know where to begin in a brief letter.

I'm enclosing a packet of information available from the embassy, along with various other leaflets and flyers I've collected in my travels and business dealings.

Why don't you call me (555-7746) to set up a lunch so we can go into greater detail?

Warmest regards,

CHARITIES, VOLUNTEER WORK, AND FUND-RAISING

Soliciting volunteer help, sponsorship, or money for charities has become almost as competitive as commercial endeavors. So your challenge in writing such a letter is to grab attention immediately. Open with a thought-provoking statement, startling question, or meaningful anecdote to entice the reader to stay with you rather than toss the request aside "to think it over."

Ask specifically for the action you want.

> *"Can you spend at least 2 days a month on the telephone to our membership?"*
>
> *"We would like to collect $200 from each family. Would that be possible on this short notice?"*
>
> *"Would you write your legislative representative to urge her support on this bill?"*

In most situations, avoid vague generalities such as "we need your support." Your effort has been wasted if readers finish your letter still wondering what *specific action* you want from them.

And because you don't have a captive audience, you must make responses easy. Give your readers all the details they need to take action: phone numbers, forms, locations, maps, or models to follow.

Remember also that people have to be assured that they are making a wise decision to devote their time or money to your cause. You can help reassure them by providing testimonials from well-known people or organizations about their enthusiasm for the cause.

Likewise, will you put your *own* money (or time) where your mouth is? Your personal commitment is always a thought in the back of a reader's mind. So don't forget to comment about your own enthusiastic support and affiliation with the charity.

As for reluctant participants, it never hurts to mention any benefits that will come to readers for responding. Will they gain publicity and recognition? Will their own family or friends benefit in some way? Will they feel fulfilled and proud of their efforts? People tune in to the WIIFM (What's in it for me?) radio station quite often these days.

COMMUNITY EVENTS

• REQUESTING RECIPIENT TO CHAIR FUND-RAISER •

Dear Mrs. Alonzo:

The Keenan Jeffries Tutorial Program desperately needs your help. Taking into consideration all your previous fund-raising experience, we are turning to you for your expertise. Mrs. Alonzo, would you please do us the honor of chairing our fund-raiser?

The K. J. Tutorial Program offers inner-city children a future by providing them with access to small-group learning that reaches beyond the standard public school curriculum. Our tutorial sessions include remedial, intermediate, and advanced education for all grade levels at no cost to the children.

We employ only certified teachers, a practice which can be expensive. Until last year, we have managed to stay solvent with contributions from parents and local businesses. However, the K. J. Tutorial Program has proved so successful that we are in danger of outgrowing our funds. Over 430 students citywide now participate in the program. We simply must hire more teachers, yet we can't afford to do so. Your positive response in chairing the effort will be our first step toward that goal.

The fund-raiser is scheduled for the entire month of September. I will contact you later in the week to discuss the drive further. If you'd like to speak with me sooner about any details, you can reach me at my office (344-588-8866) or my home (344-666-4343).

Thank you for considering the opportunity to help our kids by chairing the fund-raiser. May we count on you?

Sincerely,

• INVITING RECIPIENT TO BE GUEST SPEAKER AT FUND-RAISER •

Dear Dr. Karuum:

As you may have heard by now, the Keenan Jeffries Tutorial Program is planning a formal dinner to kick off a full month of fund-raising events. The K. J. Tutorial Program is a cause worthy of this city's fullest attention; its first-ever formal dinner merits the finest of guest speakers.

Would you, Dr. Karuum, do the K. J. Tutorial Program the honor of speaking at the dinner this September 1 at 7 p.m.? We prefer that the subject be centered on the message that education is invaluable, but within that broad guideline the subject matter is your choice. Someone of your stature in the community will lend the appropriate importance to this event.

The K. J. Tutorial Program employs only certified, degreed teachers to tutor small classes of children in any subject, at any level. The tutoring is available to those students who need help with remedial skills as well as to those who just want to learn more than is being taught during regular school hours. All tutoring is free to any student who wishes to attend. And therein lies the need for fund-raising.

Both the K. J. Tutorial Program and I would be grateful if you could help us in this endeavor. The children, too, will be grateful, and will show their appreciation by completing high school someday and continuing their academic pursuits in college. Please contact me at the phone number or address on the letterhead. We'll look forward to your positive answer.

Sincerely,

• REQUESTING RECIPIENT TO SPONSOR EVENT •

Dear Mr. Townsend:

The city of Carrera is celebrating its cultural diversity during Cultural Awareness Week, July 11–18. This is your opportunity to get some inexpensive advertising with a large audience!

One of the highlights of the weeklong celebration is the *Dance Around the Planet* performance scheduled for Wednesday, July 13, at the Carrera High School auditorium. In order to supply props, decorations, programs, and other equipment, we need businesses willing to sponsor the event.

If you will send your donation with the completed business information form enclosed with this letter, you will receive some terrific advertising in return.

Sponsorship of $100 or more earns you a 2″ × 3″ advertisement in the *Dance Around the Planet* program. Sponsorship of less than $100 reserves you a place in the alphabetical listing of sponsors on the back page.

Thank you for your continuing support of our community.

Sincerely,

• REQUESTING RECIPIENT TO SERVE ON COMMITTEE •

Example 1

Dear Mr. Dominick:

The World Watching Club is sponsoring the annual UN Day open forum discussion on October 23. We would be honored if you would consent to participate as a panelist for the discussion.

The discussion begins at 7:30 p.m. in Kendall Hall, Room 101. This year, the topic is U.S. participation in UN functions. Your extensive knowledge of peace studies would make you a distinguished addition to the panel.

Our purpose is to include as many different viewpoints as possible. We plan to form a panel with one professor from the department of economics, one from the anthropology department, one from geography, one from history, and two with differing areas of expertise from the political science department.

I will phone your office this week to confirm your participation.

Thank you,

• REQUESTING RECIPIENT TO SERVE ON COMMITTEE •

Example 2

Dear Ms. al Jared:

The Keep San Miguel Clean Committee provides the invaluable service of corralling volunteer participation from the community for local beautification projects. We are currently hoping to fill three committee-member openings.

Given your record of community involvement, we think you are the perfect choice to serve on this committee. Please consider joining us as we try to keep San Miguel beautiful.

The KSMCC heads up such projects as the semiannual San Miguel River Cleanup, in which organizations, individual citizens, and local businesses volunteer their time to pick up trash along a 6-mile stretch of the San Miguel river bank. We also work hand in hand with the city council on such beautification projects as flower- and tree-planting events, park trash-receptacle painting parties, and similar activities.

Your responsibilities would fall into the category of marketing. We need someone who can design fliers, write commercial spots for the college radio station, and write three- to four-line ads for the city newspaper.

Please respond as soon as possible. We can't wait to hear from you!

Warmest regards,

• SOLICITING BIDS FROM VENDORS •

Dear Mr. Stewart:

Our local square dance club, the Four-Squares, is sponsoring a community fund-raiser for the Turner-Selby Shelter in June. Therefore, we are soliciting bids for the print components of our campaign: a direct-mail piece, a program brochure for the closing dance, and paper placemats imprinted with information about the shelter.

If you are interested in bidding on the three projects outlined below, please submit your bid to the above address no later than April 12. An artist member of our club has prepared mock-ups of the three print pieces (enclosed) for your review in preparing your bid. We will provide camera-ready copy, but will need you to prepare the photo separations.

We've selected the paper stock and color, as noted in red ink on each mock-up. The quantities needed for each piece are also noted. Please bid the jobs separately so that we can understand what each piece is costing us, and then give us a total bid for all three jobs, including any discount that you offer if we award the contract to a single printer. If you provide any discount on such nonprofit jobs, we would appreciate knowing that also.

Because each deadline is crucial when working toward a community-announced event, we'll expect the fee to be discounted 5 percent for each day the project goes uncompleted after the agreed-upon deadline for the finished products.

Thank you for providing us with your quotation on these projects.

Sincerely,

• ACCEPTING BIDS FROM VENDORS •

Dear Mr. Wong:

We're pleased to let you know that we have selected your firm for the three printing projects involving the fund-raiser for the Turner-Selby Shelter, sponsored by the Four-Square Club.

We have accepted your total bid of $5300 and have agreed upon a completion date of April 12 for delivery of the print pieces to my home at 478 Weedon Street. You have agreed to a 3 percent discount on the total price if the print jobs are not completed by that date. We will have the camera-ready copy and all artwork/photos to you by April 1.

I've signed your quotation, with the stipulations noted above, and am enclosing a copy for your files.

We'll look forward to working with you on this project and to a successful June fund-raiser for those dependent on the Turner-Selby Shelter in their difficult times.

Sincerely,

• REMINDING PARTICIPANTS OF UPCOMING EVENT •

Dear Friends,

Just a reminder about the upcoming Neighborhood Safety Watch meeting next Tuesday, March 4, at 7:30 p.m. at Tanya and Bud Ferryman's home: 44900 Brentcroff (next to the park pavilion on the southwest corner). Mike Fuller, of the Weston Police Academy, will be speaking to our group about ways to mark and protect our property.

If you have questions about the upcoming meeting or the overall purpose of our organization, please give me a call (543-9984) so that I can give you more details.

This program to help us protect our children, ourselves, and our property deserves our full support. Can we count on you to attend the March 4 meeting?

Sincerely,

• INVITING RECIPIENTS TO ATTEND BENEFIT •

Dear Colleague:

Are you ready for an elegant evening out—complete with formal attire, gourmet food, delightful music, and an easy opportunity to help a disadvantaged youth to boot? That's right! It's time again for the annual Sundance Gala, benefiting inner-city youth.

Saturday, October 7
Hayworth Luxury Hotel
Dinner served from 7:00 to 8:30, followed by dancing

You may be wondering whose pocket will be lined with the proceeds. Each year the Sundance Gala Recipient Committee researches a number of inner-city youth programs to discover the most deserving. This year's Recipient Committee has agreed upon the Keenan Jeffries Tutorial Program. The program employs degreed teachers to tutor small classes of children in any subject, at any grade level. The tutoring is available to those students who need help with remedial skills as well as to those who just want to learn more than is being taught during regular school hours. All tutoring is free to any student who wishes to attend.

This year's fund-raising goal is $25,000. We have yet to fail to meet a fund-raising goal, and with tickets at $200 a pop ($150 without dinner), this year's goal should be a snap.

All tickets *must be purchased no later than October 1,* and may be charged by dialing (555) 555-5555. Or send a check or money order to the Sundance Gala, c/o Tickets, P.O. Box 76434, Phoenix, AZ 67544.

The weight of the world is upon us. So don your best evening wear, come hungry, and bring your checkbooks. The kids need all the help you can offer.

• ANNOUNCING UPCOMING EVENT •

Example 1

Dear Friend:

The Cherry Blossom Art Gallery is delighted to have this opportunity to invite you to the Second Annual Art for Hearts Festival. This year's showing, entitled *A Wing and a Prayer*, will showcase 12 artists and their most prominent pieces.

The more than 50 works of art range in content from the purest aesthetic simplicity to the most powerful artistic intensity. The art media range from oil and acrylic to wire and tin cans.

No admission will be charged. However, if you'd like to make a contribution, a Collector's Corner will be taking donations. All proceeds are to be donated to the St. Louis Heart Disease Research Fund.

Please return the enclosed response card indicating whether you plan to attend. We, at the Cherry Blossom Art Gallery, look forward to seeing you there.

Sincerely,

• ANNOUNCING UPCOMING EVENT •

Example 2

What could be more fun than a romp
in the cool creek on a hot spring day?

Spring Arbor DAZE
April 6–8

Snyder Park on the Square

Tickets at the Gate: Adults: $8; Children under 6: $4

We'll have—
Food: *smoked turkey legs, cotton candy, hot dogs, sundaes—
donated by local merchants*
Fun: *pony rides, cake walks, Wacky-Wack Man, roller coasters,
video games*
Fanfare: *a surprise visit from the governor, dunking booths for
council members*

**All proceeds go to the "Let's Rebuild" fund!
Call 456-9999 for details.**

• POSTPONING OR CANCELING EVENT •

Spring Arbor DAZE Postponed!

Because of the ongoing inclement weather and continued flooding, we have indefinitely postponed the April 6–8 Spring Arbor DAZE scheduled to be held on the square.

We suggest that any contributions to the "Let's Rebuild" fund be sent directly to BankFirst's account set up for that purpose: BankFirst, P.O. Box 3489, Hillsboro, OK 43711.

SOLICITING CONTRIBUTIONS

• FOR RUNAWAY CHILDREN •

Dear Mr. and Mrs. Mireliz:

Every year, 10,000 children are reported missing. Of these, a high proportion are runaways. STORC, the Shelby Trenton Organization for Runaway Children, provides vital services to both runaways and their frightened parents. But we need your help to keep those resources available.

As a nonprofit organization, STORC is always seeking donations from caring people like you. If you would like to be part of the solution, send your check or money order to the address on the letterhead.

Nationwide tracking of runaways, family counseling, construction of runaway shelters, and of course reuniting families are only a few of the resources provided by STORC. Every year we bring home hundreds of kids, and then provide them and their families with a professional counselor to help ensure lasting harmony in the home.

If you wait until tomorrow to write your check, you might forget. Do it today, and your donation may help bring a lost child home tomorrow.

Sincerely,

• FOR HOMELESS SHELTER •

Dear Concerned Resident Who Wants to Give Something Back to the Community:

The Charlotte Street Homeless Shelter needs more people! It's not more occupants we need (although our door is always open). What we need is more volunteers to help run the place!

If you think you want to engage in some tough but rewarding work, helping those who need it desperately, come join our team of volunteers. Call us any time, day or night, at 555-5555. Someone will always be available to talk with you.

We currently need volunteers to prepare meals, wash dishes, clean the bathrooms (don't worry, there are only two!), answer the phone, and be all-in-one administrators. You can work 1 hour per week—or 40 hours per week. We'll accommodate your every scheduling need.

The Charlotte Street Homeless Shelter has been in operation since 1962, when founder Karl Lincoln converted his five-bedroom home into a rent-free boardinghouse for the needy. The CSHS has since been expanded and now offers shelter to more than 3500 people each year. If you can spare the time, we can use the help.

For more information, ask for Maggie at 555-5555.

Thank you,

• FOR UNITED WAY •

Dear Concerned Citizen,

I know how valuable your time is, so I'll jump right to the point. United Way is seeking your contribution (it's tax-deductible!) to fund the huge number of volunteer and philanthropic organizations that so urgently need your help.

You may be thinking that if you decide not to contribute, your dollars won't be missed. But imagine what would become of nonprofit groups such as the American Cancer Society, Head Start, the Salvation Army, Habitat for Humanity, and others if everyone thought his or her sole contribution wouldn't make a difference. Every donation—no matter how small—counts toward putting someone's life back together.

United Way is a clearinghouse for charitable contributions. What that means is that you don't have to research different philanthropic agencies to determine which ones most merit your aid. Send your contribution to United Way and we will add it to a pool of funds that we then distribute to various nonprofit groups. With one check to United Way, you can contribute to dozens of agencies!

Enclosed is a listing of the groups that United Way serves both nationally and in our local area. Also included is a contribution form. Simply fill it out, enclose your check or money order, and return it to us. Remember to fill out and keep the bottom half for your tax records. Then give yourself a satisfactory pat on the back. You've done a good deed today.

On behalf of all our organizations, thank you for your contribution.

Sincerely,

• FOR ELEMENTARY SCHOOL LIBRARY •

Dear Parent,

Think of the one locale where you'd most like to see your child today. The Blanton Elementary School library is one of the most important places in your child's day at this stage of his or her life. Unfortunately, district funding doesn't cover all the costs of library upkeep.

The PTA has established a library fund to which you may send your contributions. Please mail your check or money order to P.O. Box 3828, Regefield, CO 80934.

If the Blanton library is to purchase more books, have old ones re-bound, acquire new chairs to replace the broken ones, install new software, and provide on-line research options, we must find another source of revenue. That source is you, the parents of the children who need to have access to the best resources possible.

Thank you for your concern and for your contribution.

Sincerely,

• FOR POLITICAL CANDIDATE •

Dear Waldon School District Resident,

Have you heard often enough from Superintendent Riley that his hands are tied? Does it seem to you that the Waldon school system has far more potential than is currently being displayed? Mao Deng could very well embody the solution for which you've been searching.

In order to develop her plans for a school system in which the actual students become the number-one priority, Mao will seek election to the school board this June. To do so, she needs not only your vote, but your campaign contribution.

Mao has planned specific projects to turn waste into productivity—to channel unnecessary cost overruns into better programs with the students' needs at heart. In the last year alone, she's authored seven pragmatic proposals designed to maximize the wealth of teacher talent in the district and the commitment of parents for volunteer time in the classroom. Five of those proposals have been adopted by the Waldon school board. The other two have been amended and are now pending passages at the next board session.

To help Waldon's schoolchildren by contributing to Mao Deng's election fund, send your contribution to P.O. Box 350, Waldon, DE 90034. You will quickly see the difference your donation makes in the future education of your children.

Thank you,

• PUBLIC SERVICE ANNOUNCEMENT •

A Public Service Announcement

Contact Frieda Frazier at 555-5555

Did you know that broccoli can actually be dangerous to your health? So can oranges, lettuce, grapes, and any other fruit or vegetable that grows on a farm. The reason? Throughout the growing season, U.S. farmers use a total of 650,000 tons of pesticides on all sorts of crops.

Please take precautions. Prepare fruits and vegetables by washing them thoroughly. Use a mild soap whenever possible. A cornsilk brush can also be helpful and is soft enough that it won't bruise food. Even frozen produce should be rinsed.

Pesticides have been known to cause birth defects and have been linked to a number of cancers. They can also aggravate allergies and contribute to a breakdown of the immune system.

If you're buying fruits and vegetables, you're probably trying to eat healthy. So don't allow the overabundance of pesticides to harm you or your family. Wash all fruits and vegetables thoroughly before you enjoy them.

Sincerely,

RESPONDING TO SOLICITATIONS

• DECLINING SOLICITATION—DISAGREE WITH CAUSE •

Dear Sam,

Without concerned citizens and volunteers, where would America be? I sincerely appreciate your efforts to beautify the city and the endless hours you have spent on various projects with that end result in mind.

However, I must disagree with your latest effort. Although installing holiday decorations along the streets and in the public parks would add cheer to the city and possibly, as you say, become a tourist attraction for the surrounding residents in smaller towns, I think our charitable contributions could be much better spent in other ways—for example, supporting our museums and libraries.

In fact, I think the holiday decorations could become a safety hazard and a cause for traffic congestion in the downtown area. For all these reasons, I will not be actively supporting this project with a contribution.

Sincerely,

• DECLINING SOLICITATION—INSUFFICIENT FUNDS •

Dear Mrs. Deng:

Our literary group was so pleased to learn of your plans to campaign for the Waldon school board seat becoming available next month. Your contributions to the district thus far during your brief two years as a resident have been invaluable.

Although our literary group supports you wholeheartedly in your attempt to gain a seat on the board, our financial committee has decided to donate all available funds to the city's public library drive for its renovation next fall.

We do wish you success in your campaign and in your ultimate efforts to ensure high-quality education for our children.

Sincerely,

VOLUNTEERING AND WORKING WITH VOLUNTEERS

• ANNOUNCING NEW SPECIAL-INTEREST GROUP •

Breast cancer is the second-leading cause of death for women over the age of 35. In order to devote special attention to this disease, I am in the process of forming ABC, Act on Breast Cancer. I'd like to enlist your help.

We need people who can volunteer their time and/or donate money. Currently, we could use your help in the following ways:

- Researching and writing articles for the newsletter
- Stuffing envelopes
- Building our database
- Raising funds from corporate sponsors

Please contact me or my cofounder, Nancy Loucks, at 555-5555. Or write us at the address on our letterhead. Even if you can't help right now but want to be added to our mailing list, I'd like to hear from you.

ABC is a nonprofit organization in its beginning stages of operation. The idea behind ABC is to empower people to fight the disease. To this end, we hope eventually to meet three goals. The first is to keep both men and women informed about the disease through a monthly newsletter. ABC's second objective is to raise awareness in the general community through publicity campaigns. Finally, we hope that ABC will eventually grow into a special-interest group that can lobby Congress for additional funding for breast cancer research.

(Continued)

I have enclosed an informative leaflet that includes some breast cancer statistics and preventive measures. Whether or not you decide to participate in ABC, please read the information and then pass it along to a friend.

Appreciatively,

• Seeking Volunteers •

Dear Member of St. Matthew's Congregation:

The Carnival Committee in charge of organizing St. Matthew's Annual Fall Carnival is seeking volunteers. We need ticket sellers and ticket takers, people to staff the stalls, and people to deck the halls!

If you want to have a festive time in the name of a worthy cause, call Lisa Barcelona (457-4499) to volunteer your services.

The Fall Carnival is St. Matt's most important source of revenue, outside of the weekly tithes and offerings of its faithful attendees. All proceeds go toward financing the winter and summer retreats, as well as minor parish repairs.

Anyone and everyone can participate in one way or another. So roll up your sleeves and get busy. Won't you put your commitment into action?

Sincerely,

• THANKING VOLUNTEERS •

Dear Nancy,

I want to express my most heartfelt gratitude to you for all your help during the MJM Scholarship fund-raising campaign. Your tireless efforts as liaison between the contributors and the university really made the difference. Your enthusiastic and thorough handling of all the details left me free to plan and manage each eventuality as it surfaced.

As for this last project, we as a team have been successful in raising more than $10,000 and are now in the final stages of receiving a presidential endowment. In addition, the university is planning a gala to kick off the scholarship. Enclosed is your personal invitation.

I hope that your services will be available to me for future projects, because I would really like to have you on my team again. Thanks again, Nancy, for all the time and effort you put into this project. I sincerely appreciate your can-do attitude and your dedication.

With warmest regards,

• RENEWING COMMITMENT OF PROJECT LEADERS •

Dear Project Leaders,

We're looking for a few good men, er, uh, women, that is. Never mind, make that ideas. We're short on plans and long on dreams. We're dreaming of achieving all those objectives set out in our first organizational meeting, but as yet we don't have specific plans from all of you, our project leaders.

Successful corporations have elaborate plans; successful individuals have elaborate plans; successful associations have elaborate plans. Concrete. Practical. Measurable. We need your input before completing our agenda for the year and setting our fee structure and budget. Success comes from the many, not the few.

Let me remind you of the issues you agreed to address as you submit your plans for your own chapter: dues, budget, charitable activities, program topics, methods for surveying potential members, and database management.

Will you let us hear from you by March 1? We're all counting on you!

Sincerely,

• VOLUNTEERING FOR SPECIAL PROGRAM OR COMMITTEE •

Dear Mr. Rammal,

I heard a public service announcement on the radio today, asking for volunteers for your remedial-reading tutorials. I would very much like to offer my services but am a bit unsure about my skills in this area.

Please send me some information regarding the program in general and volunteer duties in particular.

I have plenty of questions: Do you train the volunteers? During which hours would I be needed? Of what ages and grade levels are your students? Is there a minimum time requirement for volunteers?

I am really excited about this opportunity, both for myself and for the children your tutoring program reaches. I look forward to hearing from you.

Sincerely,

• DECLINING REQUEST FOR VOLUNTEERS •

Dear Amy:

The children said you phoned last night, asking about my availability to work at one of the polling sites for the school board elections at the end of the month. With the sporadic voter turnout in off-election years, I can imagine how difficult it must be to anticipate how many volunteers you will actually need on election day.

Because of the unpredictability of my children's soccer games on Saturday, I've decided to reduce our family frustration level by not taking on any additional Saturday commitments of my time this year. I think it would be easier for all concerned to say no up front rather than have to cancel at the last minute.

Thank you for your own efforts on behalf of the school district. I'll be hoping for good weather and a good voter turnout.

Cordially,

• RESIGNING FROM VOLUNTEER POSITION •

Dear Alex,

As you know, I have been the volunteer Spanish-English media liaison for the Soccer Cup for four years running. I have enjoyed the work immensely, and I consider this an important role to the Soccer Cup organization. For those reasons, I regret to tell you that I must resign my post.

I am giving you two months' notice with the hope that you will have time to find another bilingual sports aficionado to handle the job. I suggest that you begin your search for a replacement in the communications department of the local college.

Having begun a new job this year, I find that the demands of my travel and work schedule simply prohibit my spending the time necessary to your organization. If circumstances permit, perhaps I will be able to volunteer for the Soccer Cup organization again in the future. You have my very best wishes for another exciting year.

Best regards,

CLERGY AND SUPPORT ORGANIZATIONS

Members of the clergy and support organizations often are over-looked for their efforts because their help is perceived to be "just their job." Nevertheless, these people deserve our thanks for actions and attitudes that extend beyond what's expected.

So take every occasion to express your appreciation for the clergy and support services available to you and the community.

"I want to express my gratitude for…"

"Thank you for your expression of concern when you visited my mother in the hospital before her death."

"You have made a meaningful contribution to my life, and I wanted to let you know how much I appreciate your time."

Often, people think they are giving a stronger commendation when they are global in their comments, such as "You are always so supportive." Actually, just the opposite is true. A specific, rather than global, commendation sounds more sincere. Comment specifically on what the person has done that was so meaningful or special to you or your family or the community.

Remember, also, that individuals—not institutions—do meaning-ful, sacrificial work. So comment on the individual's personal dedica-tion to the service he or she provides and the people served. For example:

"You have demonstrated remarkable commitment."

"Your personal sacrifice is very evident to observers."

"Your personal warmth shines through the community role you play."

"Your genuine goodwill and personal concern are evident."

If you are writing to ask for help, be sure to make your request for any action specific. And provide all details to make the requested action easy to take (for example, copies of past correspondence or phone numbers and addresses of people you wish to be contacted on your behalf).

Finally, remember that members of the clergy have the same need for emotional support and recognition and the same family and individual concerns as other members of society. Show your appreciation accordingly and often.

• WELCOMING NEW CLERGY TO CONGREGATION •

Dear Reverend Salm,

My family and I are so happy that you've come to settle in the Guiding Light Parish at Clearwoods, Virginia. Although I plan to introduce myself to you in person after the worship services this weekend, I didn't want you to spend a whole week in your new town without receiving a welcome from someone.

We've all heard such wonderful things about you from Reverend Greg. He speaks very highly of your academic credentials as well as your commitment to establish programs in the parish that benefit the whole family. Even though we are sad to see him go, I think we all consider ourselves fortunate to have you join us here to serve God in our little corner of the world.

I look forward to meeting you in person.

Sincerely,

• WELCOMING NEW SERVICE ORGANIZATION •

Dear Mr. and Mrs. Sanatti,

Welcome to Greenburgh. My wife and I are overjoyed that you have decided to establish a chapter of Kid-Tracker here. Your presence will relieve part of our fear that one day the worst could happen—that not only could we lose our child, but we would then have nowhere to turn for help and comfort.

As soon as the local chapter of Kid-Tracker is up and running, we plan to bring in our two sons and one daughter for fingerprinting and photo records. Everything we as parents and ministers can do to protect our children certainly merits our time and attention.

We are aware of the success that you've had in other communities, and I'm sure that that will be the case here as well. You two must be very caring individuals to have committed all your spare time to this important support service.

Sincerely,

• EXPRESSING APPRECIATION TO CLERGY •

For Sermon

Dear Father Teal:

I want to be the first to tell you what a wonderful sermon you preached last Sunday. I was touched by your message, and am deeply grateful for the hope and faith that you inspired in me.

This last year has been a difficult one for me, and I sometimes find myself questioning God's wisdom, if not His existence. Some comments that you made the other day about trying to hang on to one's faith really hit home. So did your advice on how to maintain and strengthen one's relationship with God. Your words encouraged me to see the world, my purpose, and my life in a different light.

It's important to me that you know that you did reach someone. I am deeply appreciative for your hours of study and your capable delivery of God's word.

All my thanks,

• EXPRESSING APPRECIATION TO CLERGY •

For Baptism

Dear Minister Carver:

The baptismal ceremony in which you baptized our granddaughter, Elizabeth Martin, last week was both meaningful and inspiring. Thank you for marking the beginning of my granddaughter's walk with God such a memorable event for her and the family.

Your comments during the ceremony fully explained to all present the significance of such a symbolic act. I especially appreciate your time spent in visiting with Elizabeth both before and after the ceremony to help her understand fully that commitment at this time in her life. In keeping with your message, my husband and I will do our best to further her growth as she applies her knowledge of the scripture to her daily life.

When Elizabeth was born, we promised that we'd dedicate her to the Lord's service, and we intend to continue with that commitment. We feel fortunate that our family has you as leader and counselor in our church and community.

Sincerely,

• EXPRESSING APPRECIATION TO CLERGY •

For Sympathy and Support

Dear Pastor Allen,

As you know, this last month has been a very difficult time for my family and me. Brian's sudden diagnosis and hospitalization took us all by surprise. Your comfort in our time of need was greatly appreciated then, as it is now.

Thank you so much for visiting Brian and us at the hospital. Your frequent presence there was a constant reminder of God's care and the congregation's concern, even when times seemed hopeless.

You'll be happy to know that Brian has been released from the hospital and is resting comfortably at home. If he maintains his regimen, the doctors predict a slow but full recovery. Thank you for giving so freely of your time in our time of need.

Warmest regards,

• EXPRESSING APPRECIATION TO CLERGY •

For Holiday Service

Dear Pastor Fendley:

I want to commend you on a job well done. Last Sunday's Easter service was beautiful to observers, inspiring to the participants, and meaningful to all of us as a reminder of the historical event and religious significance we celebrate.

Obviously, you and your staff spent long hours in planning the service, selecting the appropriate music, coordinating the visuals and media support, and preparing the message. After 40 to 60 hours in the world of work every week, we members of the congregation appreciate a chance to get away from the hustle and bustle and reflect on our higher purpose in life. You provided that opportunity once again Sunday, and I thank you.

Sincerely,

• REQUESTING PERSONAL CHARACTER REFERENCE •

Dear Reverend Hornsby,

I am in the process of updating my résumé and would like to include some new reference letters as I begin my job search. Would you be willing to provide a character reference letter for me? If so, you can simply address it "To Whom It May Concern" and send it to me at my home address listed on the church records.

As you are probably aware, corporations have become increasingly concerned about the character and temperament of their potential employees. With violence in the workplace growing and unethical behavior a blot on any company's record, prospective employers want to know that those they're considering for hire are honest, trustworthy, and stable individuals.

Just as a reminder of my work in the church, I began attending the Eternal Light Church in 1994. During my time here, I have involved myself in a number of church activities, including volunteering for the monthly brunch for newcomers, working during the clothing drive, and sponsoring several youth events and trips.

For your convenience, I am enclosing a copy of my résumé so that you have a better idea about the kind of position I'm seeking and can tailor your comments accordingly. Thank you for taking the time to provide this reference.

Sincerely,

• REQUESTING COUNSELING FROM CLERGY (FOR FRIEND) •

Dear Pastor Soledad,

A very good friend of mine is in trouble. He is depressed, and I no longer feel as though I can handle the problem on my own. He has agreed (with much prodding on my part) to seek counseling, and I recommended you to him.

Could you please work him into your busy schedule as soon as possible? If so, please let me know your available appointment times and I'll arrange for him to be there. It's not that he is unwilling to come for counseling; it's that his depression has left him in a very lethargic mood and I fear he'll not take the initiative to call himself.

His name is Chris Madero, and he lost his wife about a year ago. She had had a lengthy disease, and needless to say, Chris was devastated by her death. Six months later, however, he began dating an old acquaintance (who incidentally just lost her father). They are planning to marry and I'm afraid that, in their vulnerable, grief-stricken states, they are rushing into something they are not ready for.

Neither of them appears to be really happy with their wedding plans, but I don't think that they have the strength of will to change or postpone them either. It seems that they both need something positive to cling to. I hope that you can help them.

You can reach me during the day at 415-7849 or in the evenings at 899-9944 about available appointment times. Thanks so much for making your expertise open to the community.

Sincerely,

• REQUESTING COUNSELING FROM CLERGY (FOR YOURSELF) •

Dear Father Nguyn:

Lately things have been difficult for me. Although I don't feel acute depression, I simply have trouble finding meaning and keeping interested in activities that I used to find enjoyable.

Being rather unfamiliar with the working of the church behind the scenes, I'm unsure if you offer counseling to nonmembers of your congregation. (I attend, but am not a member.) If so, how do I go about scheduling an appointment? Do you charge for such personal counseling? Or could you recommend someone who might offer me some advice and/or peace of mind?

Let me give you a little background: A little over a year ago, I lost a very good friend in a car accident. She was the mother of three beautiful girls and the wife of a loving husband. Since the accident, I have seen the remainder of the family fall apart over their grief. I myself am consumed with the idea that the same thing will happen to our family someday. It seems ridiculous that I should be so concerned with such notions; nevertheless, I am beside myself with these thoughts.

I don't know where else to turn, because our financial situation is such that I cannot afford counseling from a private clinic or counselor. Having attended your church for so long, I have come to trust your judgment. I'd appreciate your call (477-3349), suggesting the next step in dealing with this issue.

Sincerely,

• INVITING CLERGY TO BE GUEST SPEAKER •

Dear Reverend Daimler,

I am a member of a wonderful support group for the adult children of terminally ill parents. Once a week we meet on the Wakefield University campus to share coping ideas, encouragement, and inspiration. Whenever possible, we like to hear speakers as well. They can be particularly helpful on the days when we just can't seem to inspire ourselves.

Reverend Daimler, I think you'd be the perfect speaker for such an event. Would you consider attending one of our upcoming meetings (Wednesday, June 15, would be terrific) to speak to this group, which so desperately needs your guidance? You are free to choose any topic. The meeting participants practice a wide range of religions; so if at all possible, I recommend that your comments be ecumenical.

We meet every Wednesday at 7 p.m. in the Kasha Room in the Everett Library. I've enclosed a map to help you find your way around the Wakefield campus. If you decide that you can find the time to speak to our group, I need a couple of days' notice so we can plan accordingly. And if you'd like to attend a meeting beforehand to get a feel for the group, please feel free to drop in.

I realize that you have many demands on your time and will understand if you cannot speak to our group. If your answer is positive, I'll appreciate a call at 478-9985. On behalf of the whole group, thank you for considering our need for an encouraging message.

Sincerely,

P.S. As you may have guessed, we have no budget at all. We don't accept dues or donations (except for time), so we cannot afford to pay our speakers. Even under those circumstances, we hope to hear from you.

COLLEGE

Consider almost any communication to or about colleges as a business letter rather than the typical personal letter. Even though you may be requesting references from friends, your request will generally get a higher priority and you will write a more authoritative, formal reference if you model a business tone in your request.

Summarize your message or request immediately in the opening sentence or two.

> *"I'm writing to ask that you furnish a reference for..."*
>
> *"Would you be willing to write a letter of reference to help me..."*
>
> *"I'd like to ask you for a reference letter, if you would feel comfortable providing one for me on the basis of our past association..."*

Then provide all details relative to the situation: full name with initials, dates of past or future attendance, deadlines, fees, identification such as social security number or student number, field of study, future plans, and so forth. Here are some lead-ins that you might find helpful in jogging your reader's mind:

> *"Let me refresh your memory a bit about my work."*
>
> *"As I'm sure you may recall, we both..."*
>
> *"Let me summarize some of the details of our past association that would be of particular interest to a potential employer."*

Such prompts will ensure that your reader provides the kind of information that will be useful for landing the job, scholarship, or award.

Enclosing a self-addressed, stamped envelope if you are asking for a written action on your behalf is also a thoughtful gesture that helps ensure a prompt response forwarded to the appropriate person without misrouting.

REFERENCES AND INTRODUCTIONS

• REQUESTING REFERENCES •

Dear Dr. Gorman:

I am applying for the Presidential Scholarship, a $5000 annuity to be awarded to a single student. Given that my attendance at Southwestern University is dependent on my receiving financial aid, this is a wonderful opportunity for me.

Would you do me the honor of submitting one of the two reference letters that are required for application? The recipient of the Presidential Scholarship must demonstrate both ability and direction in his or her field of study. In order to assess such qualities, the Scholarship Committee requires that applicants submit reference letters from two professors in their major department.

I took your International Law class in the fall semester of 1996 and your International Organization class in the spring of 1997. I received an A in both classes.

All scholarship materials must be submitted by March 1, and I have enclosed an addressed, stamped envelope for your convenience. I will be stopping by your office during your conference hours this week to confirm. In the meantime, if you need to speak with me for any reason, please call me at (512) 555-5555. Thank you for your time in providing this reference.

Appreciatively,

• SUPPLYING REFERENCES •

Dear Dr. Augustine,

One of my students, Andy Swift, is making application to the Presidential Scholarship Committee for that award. It is my opinion that Mr. Swift is an excellent candidate for the award in question; he has proved himself well qualified in every facet of the scholarship requirements, both in my classes and elsewhere.

Having served as a college professor in the St. Luke's system for several years, I have had the opportunity to notice a few students who really stand out from the rest. Andy Swift is one of these rare students. He has demonstrated dedication and serious attention to academic achievement. He has an excellent attitude and work ethic, which will no doubt form the foundation for his success in college.

In my classes with Mr. Swift—namely, macroeconomics and international finance—he has exhibited both creativity and deep insight, far beyond his years, into the world of finance. We at St. Luke's have recognized him a number of times for academic excellence and achievement in various extracurricular activities.

In addition, Mr. Swift is involved in a number of school and community activities that further demonstrate his wide range of interests and his ceaseless energy. He is currently the president of Sigma Iota Rho, the international studies organization; he is an instructional assistant for the Spanish department; and he volunteers for the Feed Birmingham program in his "spare" time.

I might add that I am aware of other professors' opinions regarding Mr. Swift, and to my knowledge, they are in accordance with mine. That is, Andy Swift is the superior choice for recipient of the Presidential Scholarship.

Sincerely,

• INTRODUCING CHILD OR FRIEND APPLYING TO COLLEGE •

Dear Dr. Dunn:

As I know you are aware, it is that time of year when students begin competing with one another to gain acceptance into the university of their choice. My daughter, herself soon to graduate from Bowie High School in Plano, plans to apply to Texas Christian University next month. Her name is Meaghan MacKenzie, and as I understand it, she is well qualified by TCU's admissions standards.

Having worked as an administrative professional in a Dallas-based consulting firm for more than 10 years, I believe it within my capacity to recognize ability in people. And in Meaghan I see someone who possesses certain qualities that, if cultivated under the proper instruction, will lead to a fulfilling and successful career in medicine.

Meaghan has exhibited both scholarship and direction as a high school student. Her marks are above average; she holds a grade point average of 11 on a scale of 14. And this May she will graduate in the top 15 percent of Bowie High School's senior class. In addition, she is involved in a number of extracurricular activities, such as the French Club, the Drama Club, Circle K (the volunteer organization), and dance classes and performances.

May we count on you to give her guidance as she seeks to add her name to the freshman roster at TCU? She'll be phoning your office next week to check the status of her application. In the meantime, you can reach her at (214) 489-0986. Her complete admissions package is enclosed.

Sincerely,

• INTRODUCING STUDENT APPLYING TO COLLEGE •

Dear Dr. Ito:

I want to take this opportunity to introduce you to one of my best students, Michael Phillips. As I am sure you will agree after you meet him, he would make a valuable addition to Green Bay's student body.

As an English teacher in the Madison school system for more than 10 years, I pride myself on recognizing and encouraging exceptional scholarship in my pupils. And in Michael, I see unlimited potential. He is bright, energetic, and a serious student.

In my classes with Michael, he has exhibited both maturity and commitment to excellence in his assignments. As a student in general, his marks are above the norm. He holds a GPA of 3.5 on a 4.0 scale, and this May will graduate in the top 10 percent of his class.

In addition, he is involved in a number of extracurricular activities. This year alone he has performed leading roles in both Bowie's fall and spring plays. Also active on the student council, Michael often brings fresh ideas for new activities to the meetings. And in his precious free time, he plays soccer for a city league.

In conclusion, I would like to add that although Michael has received very little emotional support and encouragement from his family, he is a responsible young man who is well liked by his teachers and friends. He plans to major in political science. I know he will be an outstanding student at Green Bay.

Sincerely,

• DECLINING TO SUPPLY REFERENCE •

Dear Janelle,

Thank you for considering me as a source for references as you apply for admission and a scholarship to the University of Alabama.

Of course, I've known your parents for years through various projects in the community, but I'm afraid my knowledge of your own academic abilities, character, and goals is extremely limited. Although I'd be happy to comment about the fine relationship I have with your parents, I hesitate to pass judgment on someone I've had very little association with at all. Therefore, I suggest that you find someone who could give you a much stronger reference than I.

As you know, the University of Alabama is also my alma mater, and I'm still very active in the alumni association. I think you've made a fine choice of universities, and I wish you the best there in your academic pursuits.

Sincerely,

REQUESTS FOR INFORMATION

• REQUESTING INFORMATION FOR APPLICATION •

Dear Mr. Ceiplik,

I am a senior at Stanton High School and plan to graduate in May of this year. It is my intent to attend Northwestern University the following autumn. My major is as yet undecided, though I do have an interest in Spanish and in history.

Please send me an application for admission to NWU and the current spring catalog, as well as the spring schedule of classes as soon as it becomes available. I would also appreciate any additional information you might offer history and Spanish majors.

Can you also provide financial-aid information? (Or possibly route my letter to the correct department for that information?) I am not sure about my eligibility for grants, loans, and/or scholarships. So if you could please send me any relevant information about those requirements too, I would be grateful.

Thank you,

• REQUESTING INFORMATION ABOUT SON'S OR DAUGHTER'S PERFORMANCE •

RE: Student Dalton Andrew Cominsky
    Social Security Number 123-45-6789

Dear Dr. Aligalani:

I'm trying to evaluate more thoroughly the performance of my son (Dalton Andrew Cominsky) at your university this year. Although I do receive reports on his final grades, I prefer to be informed on a more regular basis about his general adjustment. As both a freshman and a wheelchair-bound student, he has experienced some difficulty on campus that I'd like to verify.

I would be extremely grateful if you could compile whatever details with regard to his performance that you deem pertinent. I am mostly concerned with his attendance, his professors' opinions about his general attitude, and of course his grades. Is he enthusiastic? Does he appear to be enjoying his classes specifically? Is the work too difficult for him, or does he not exert enough effort?

Dalton entered GMU in the fall of last year as a finance major. Since receiving his grades for the fall semester, I have become very concerned with Dalton's future at the university. You and I are both aware of the pitfalls into which a first-year university student may tumble if he's not careful. Additionally, as you may surmise, his physical condition sometimes limits his potential for social interactions. As a parent, I want to make sure he practices good study habits and that he feels fully welcome among the student body.

Please send all available information and your collective observations to me at the above address. Thank you for your help in this endeavor.

Sincerely,

• REQUESTING TRANSCRIPT •

To the Director of Transcripts:

I am applying to graduate school and so would like to request an official transcript to be sent to the School of Graduate Studies at the University of Nevada, Las Vegas. The address is as follows:

University of Nevada, Las Vegas
School of Graduate Studies Admissions
P.O. Box 4483
Las Vegas, NV 38543-4483

My name as it appears on the transcript is Alejandra L. Palermo (social security/student identification number: 555-55-5555). I graduated in May 19— with a BA in psychology.

Please charge the cost of sending the transcript to my Visa card (9876-5432-2345-6789; expiration date: 11/99).

Thank you,

DECLINING ATTENDANCE AND WITHDRAWING

• DECLINING ATTENDANCE •

Dear Dr. LaFleur:

I would like to thank you for your decision to accept me as a transfer student from Mountainview Junior College. However, I have decided to attend another university because of the generous financial-aid package offered to me there.

I appreciate your taking the time to review my application, and I have the highest regard for your university. Best wishes for your continued success.

Sincerely,

• CHANGING MAJOR OR WITHDRAWING FROM PROGRAM •

RE: Forester Grover
    Student ID 493-44-5556

Dear Dr. Salazar,

I intend to withdraw from the International Relations program for international studies majors at this end of the spring semester of this year. I have decided to pursue an alternative course of study; therefore, I will no longer be studying within your department.

Please make the necessary modifications to my record. I must be officially released by you from the International Relations program before I can register for the next semester under a different major.

I will be changing my major to modern languages. Although I have enjoyed studying the theory connected with international studies, I believe that fluency in a foreign language will be of more practical use to me in the career field that I have chosen to pursue.

Good luck to you and your department. Thank you for the education you've provided me in these last two semesters.

Sincerely,

RESOLVING CONFLICTS WITH TEACHERS AND ADMINISTRATION

• REQUESTING REINSTATEMENT AFTER DISCIPLINARY ACTION •

Dear Dr. Heudier:

I would like to be reinstated at the university, both as graduate teaching assistant and as coordinator of the Instructional Assistantship program. It has been nearly nine months since I relinquished my teaching role and withdrew from my graduate studies. Perhaps your decision and mine were made too hastily.

I urge you to reconsider the situation. If you'll recall, my grades were not the problem; my attendance was sporadic. Unusual family circumstances at that time prevented me from fulfilling my teaching duties and devoting full time to my graduate studies to the best of my ability. These family difficulties have been resolved, and I feel certain that I can now give my full attention to the job and to my graduate studies.

I would like to make an appointment with you to discuss reinstatement and will phone you within the next week. I will be happy to make myself available to you at any time so that we may discuss the matter in greater detail. For now, suffice it to say that my personal life will not interfere with my career again.

For your convenience in reexamining my credentials or conversing with my present employer, I have enclosed a current résumé, along with a copy of my transcript at the time of withdrawal. Thank you for the courtesy of your reconsideration.

Sincerely,

• REQUESTING DORM TRANSFER •

RE: Chaundra Sue Smith
Social Security Number 578-54-5555

Dear Mr. Mizrahi:

With this letter, I am requesting a dormitory transfer. I am aware that midterm transfers are unusual, but undue circumstances make this transfer a necessity. Life at Laurel Hall is not conducive to good study habits, and if I am to do well in my classes this semester, I must relocate immediately.

Both my resident assistant and the hall director are aware of my decision and have given me their approval. Please make whatever arrangements that you can to grant the transfer and then notify them or me. My resident assistant's name is Tanya Schoon; the hall director's name is Stephanie Charros. Both can be reached after 4 p.m. at 456-9934.

As a sophomore who has completed 45 hours of credit classes, I prefer to move into Butler Hall or the Women's Resident Tower. Butler Hall is preferable, because I would like to remain in the same price range as Laurel Hall.

Most of the women in Laurel Hall are freshmen, whereas I have begun to take upper-level classes. They still have the time and the energy to stay up until all hours talking and listening to music. I, on the other hand, have to put in more time on my schoolwork, so I find their late-night chatter disruptive. They are not excessively noisy; they are just bothersome to anyone trying to study.

I will appreciate whatever you can do to help make my living quarters more conducive to study.

Respectfully yours,

• DISPUTING UNFAIR GRADE •

Dear Dr. Tran:

I'm sure that the most tiresome words a professor can hear at the end of a term are, "I think my grade is wrong." Unfortunately, I really do think mine has been miscalculated.

I had been making B's all semester in your class, yet my final grade report shows a C. Would you please check your records to verify accuracy? I will call you next week for the results.

I was in your class in Economics 4353, Money and Banking, Section 001, which met MWF at 10 a.m. My student ID number is 555-55-5555. My full name is William S. Jamal.

Enclosed are copies of the front pages of all tests and papers from the class (with the grade recorded in your own writing), as well as my official final grade report. If you wish to speak with me about this before I phone you, you can reach me at 555-5555.

Thanks for your investigation of what I hope turns out to be an honest mistake.

Respectfully,

• DISPUTING UNFAIR DISCIPLINARY ACTION •

Dear Chairwoman Richards,

Two weeks ago several of my friends and I were reported for drinking in our dorm room; the subsequent hearing with the disciplinary board is scheduled for March 12. I want to make sure that the board is aware of the special circumstances before that date. Perhaps the board will decide that this case isn't worth hearing. Or perhaps having this information in advance will make the hearing proceed more quickly.

It would be futile to deny that we were drinking. But please consider the circumstances: we were sharing a bottle of champagne given to one of the girls by her parents. The girl, who was also written up, is Cecilia Guitierrez. While at home over the weekend, she and her boyfriend had become engaged to be married and her parents had given her the champagne to celebrate with her friends. When Ceci returned to the dorm Sunday night, she shared her bottle of champagne with seven of us to celebrate her engagement.

We are all aware of the regulations with regard to drinking on campus. Needless to say, we have all learned our lesson. As you are aware, if the case is not thrown out by the disciplinary board, it will become a mark on our permanent records, and none of us seven has any previous disciplinary infraction. We hope that, upon closer reexamination, you will decide that this one act of poor judgment on our part doesn't merit marring our otherwise excellent records.

Respectfully,

CONGRATULATIONS

Look for opportunities to congratulate others on their accomplishments or happy occasions. Congratulatory notes can nurture a casual acquaintance into a full-blooming friendship. And for those who are already friends, special events take on added significance when shared and recognized by those we care about and love.

With that in mind, offer your immediate congratulations on the event, award, honor, or occasion. Be as informal or "gushy" as your friendship allows. If you're pleased, say so; if you're surprised, say so; if you're thrilled, let your emotions show.

Be specific with your comments. Why exactly does the person deserve the recognition or reward? Your specific praising comments give the reader time to "enjoy" the event or honor once again.

> *"I heard you completed the entire marathon in the top 10!"*
>
> *"Betsy tells me that you were selected for the honor among competition that included more than 400 peers. That's phenomenal."*
>
> *"I understand that you had to give over 250 presentations to win this distinction. What a feat!"*

The other person wants to know for sure that you understand the difficulties in any achievement, the honor in any award, or the pleasure in any event.

Be personal and genuine. Avoid a tone that sounds global, vague, and boilerplate with clichéd statements and sentiments. If a particular phrase seems to "roll off your tongue," that's a good sign that it is a clichéd expression. Try to reword the sentiment with less familiar phrasing.

Your personal note demonstrates that you're the kind of friend or associate who feels excitement and pride rather than jealousy when someone else receives recognition or experiences happy occasions.

• ANNIVERSARY •

Margo and Kevin,

Rumor has it that you two have spent 20 wonderful years together. Congratulations on having chosen your life's partner so well, for growing more in love through the years, and for being a role model for the rest of the world. In this day and age, marriages like yours should never be taken for granted, and I wanted to take this opportunity to wish you both continued love and happiness together. Have a special celebration.

Cordially,

• BAR MITZVAH •

Dear Paul,

I am so proud of you. You have grown into a terrific young man, and you truly deserve this day and all the recognition it involves.

The way I hear it, you've been studying very hard (*every night!*) to make your Bar Mitzvah readings and recitations perfect. You'll do wonderfully well in school and in life because that is how you do things—with attention to the details and with full enthusiasm.

Congratulations, kiddo. (I have to call you "kiddo" this one last time because after this weekend you'll be too grown-up.) Soon you'll be a man. And nothing could make me prouder or happier for you. This weekend marks a significant event in your life and in the life of our family.

Best wishes,

• BIRTH •

Mina and Raphael,

The long nights walking the floor, the cross-country vacations with stops every half hour, the babysitters who set *your* curfews—your lives will soon be changing. But, of course, there will also be sticky hugs and kisses, starring roles in school performances that will make you proud, and late-night chat sessions about boyfriends. Life will change for the better and for the best. Congratulations on your precious baby daughter! Please continue to keep us up to date on the happenings in your lives.

Our best wishes,

• BIRTHDAY •

Rachel,

It's your day! Take a long walk in the sunlight. Eat a banana split. Hug somebody special. Birthdays should excite, thrill, and inspire you. You've made a good start, because all those people in my corner of the world are wishing you a terrific celebration. You are special to us. Keep counting.

Love,

• ENGAGEMENT OR WEDDING •

Sarah,

I've just heard the wonderful news—that you've found the love of your life. Timothy must be a brilliant man, a gentle and caring man, an ambitious man—and a very wise man. He would have to be all those things to attract someone like you. We're so happy for you. Enjoy each other's love every day for the rest of your lives.

Sincerely,

• GRADUATION •

Heather,

Graduation marks a significant milestone in life. But the best of everything is yet to come. We know you've worked hard, made excellent grades, and enjoyed many extracurricular activities to develop the skills and attitudes that will continue to make you successful in life. You have our best wishes as you take on the world ahead of you. We are very proud of you.

Cordially,

• OPENING OWN BUSINESS •

Dear Madison:

Congratulations on opening your own import-export business! You've accomplished what most people only spend their time talking about—real control over your life and your future.

Back in April when the government threw all that red tape at you, I know how tempted you were just to give up. But true to form, you stuck with it (even when the airlines lost your first shipment of jewelry!), and I know that you now feel all that difficulty has been worth the price of a promising future.

I have every confidence in your success and am so happy for you. Please keep me updated on your progress. I'll be looking forward to sending customers your way.

Regards,

• PERSONAL ACCOMPLISHMENT •

Well look at *you!* Here you are at age "40-something" and going after your master's degree. It takes courage to do what you've done in switching careers (not to mention endless energy). I want you to know that I admire your risk-taking mindset.

I'm also proud of you for standing up to the criticisms that I know you've received from your family. I guess for some people, education is something to finish and put behind them. I know that for you, getting your MA has more significance than the diploma itself. It represents research into complex new theories, intelligent searching for self-fulfillment, and solid determination to prepare yourself for a new career in service to others.

Good luck to you in this and all the future goals you set for yourself. You're an excellent role model for all of us.

Sincerely,

• PROMOTION •

Example 1

Dear Brad:

I understand that you've just been appointed vice president in charge of production for the Commercial Film Institute. And the way I hear it, you were more than a little surprised. But I'm sure that no one deserves the honor more than you do.

Your past awards and commercial film successes testify to your extraordinary talent. It must be wonderful to be recognized by your colleagues as well, for the very same qualities.

Congratulations on your appointment. It's a fabulous opportunity and I have no doubt you'll create all kinds of new opportunities for all of us in the industry as you fulfill your new leadership role.

My best regards,

• Promotion •

Example 2

Dear Merisha,

I've heard a rumor that turned out to be true for a change—you've been promoted! Congratulations. Am I correct to assume you didn't know about it back when we met for dinner in Sacramento?

In any case, the higher-ups couldn't have made a better choice. We all watched as you almost single-handedly pulled in the Sampson account. Dedication like that deserves to be recognized. I'm glad to see that people get what they deserve in this company. Creativity, good ideas, and hard work really do pay off in your case.

Good luck in your new capacity as director of new accounts.

• PUBLIC RECOGNITION •

Dear Mrs. Paul,

It is a wonderful moment when a teacher and administrator as dedicated as you are receives the recognition she deserves. I saw the Channel 8 coverage on you and your career in the Fairview public school system several weeks ago and have been meaning to get in touch with you ever since.

You were my sixth-grade homeroom teacher in 1990. I recall that, even back then, you were the kind of person who knows how to motivate. Children can tell when an adult really cares about them, and you demonstrated that concern to us years ago, as you obviously do now.

If anyone deserves recognition for framing young minds, it's you. Thank you for caring. Thank you for teaching. I'm glad Channel 8 took the initiative in spotlighting your career and contribution to the community. Congratulations.

Warmest regards,

• PUBLICATION IN NEWSPAPER OR JOURNAL •

Dear Kim:

Someone mentioned to me that you are actually going to have a paper published in *ABD Journal*. Congratulations! You had mentioned to me that you are involved in a research program that's centered around the connection between cancer and nutrition. But I had no idea your concepts and theories were so innovative.

I am anxious to read the article. During our brief group discussion at the party, I was titillated. You really have a mesmerizing delivery, even when you are just *talking* about your research. No doubt that quality comes through bright and clear in your writing. No wonder the publishers selected your work for publication.

The subject of the cancer-nutrition link is well timed too. I am thrilled that someone with your qualifications has spent the kind of time that such an important subject merits. Good luck with your future research.

Regards,

CONSUMER ISSUES AND CONCERNS

As a consumer, you experience both excellent and poor service. And both should be occasions for writing letters to make organizations aware of exceptional employees—and terrible situations and service.

For the excellent dinner service, for the superb flight in which an attendant took extra care of your traveling loved one, for the special furniture delivery during the rainstorm, you want to express your appreciation immediately. Comment specifically on what the service personnel did to make you feel special or to make your purchase exceptional. Were they quick, efficient, thoughtful, thorough, sensitive? And remember to include names of individuals, not just departments or groups. With a name, the organization that receives your letter can relay your praise to the exact person who deserves it. Often such letters mean raises or recognition.

As for the poor meal, for the flight in which all rights were ignored and needs minimized, and for the furniture damaged during delivery, you need to complain so that your letter gets action.

First, summarize the situation or problem briefly up front. Include enough of the details so that readers can quickly grasp what has happened. Don't assume that they will "fill in the details" about the severity or difficulty of a situation. Often those who receive the complaint letters are far removed from the day-to-day scene.

Then be specific about the action or adjustment you expect on a problem situation. Use a confident, not angry, tone. Avoid sarcasm if your ultimate objective is to have a problem corrected as you wanted it to be handled. Sarcasm and threats tend to lessen others' motivation for resolving a problem expeditiously.

"We are confident that you see the situation from our point of view."

"We're looking forward to improved service the next trip."

"I'm assuming the new shipment will arrive promptly."

"Thank you for giving this situation your immediate and full attention. We hope you can restore our confidence in your organization."

Don't forget to enclose all necessary paperwork (receipts, past orders or letters, canceled checks, catalog numbers, merchandise labels, warranties, service agreements, and so forth).

APPRECIATION

• TECHNICAL SUPPORT •

Dear Viola,

I cannot thank you enough for the flawless technical support that you've given me over the last couple of months.

The slides that you created for the Glazton presentation were a big hit; and the multimedia extravaganza unfolded on cue with perfect precision. My colleagues were as impressed with *me* as I am with *you*. You also did a marvelous job researching the report (and I know that I didn't always give you much to go on) and recommending exactly the appropriate graphics software for their preferences.

Without your help, I don't think I could have met the short but urgent deadline. I feel much better knowing that I have such a valuable and capable resource a phone call away.

Regards,

• HELPFUL SALESPERSON •

Dear Mr. Cerwins:

I would like to commend you on the excellence of your sales staff. I was in your store Saturday afternoon, December 26; and given the number of customers who were shopping there that day, I expected less than your best service. To my surprise and pleasure, Kenny McKnight, one of your salespeople, provided exactly the help I needed with an exchange.

Having received a Sony portable compact disc player for Christmas that I didn't need, I set out to your store to return it the following day. Expecting the worst because of the after-Christmas sales, I fought my way through the crowds of holiday shoppers to look for the correct counter to return the purchase. Apparently, I looked as frustrated as I felt, because Kenny greeted me and then guided me to the correct counter to get a refund on the player. But that was not the end of his effort. The replacement model that I wanted was out of stock. Again, Kenny spent more than half an hour calling your other stores to locate the appropriate model. During our discussion, I was also delighted by his in-depth product knowledge, something of a rarity in this self-serve era.

Obviously, you know how to train and motivate people, so I expect that Kenny will receive the attention that he deserves as a result of my writing today.

I will definitely be shopping at your store again, primarily because of the high-quality service and attention I received there on a very busy day.

Cordially,

• HONEST MECHANIC •

Dear Jay:

I would like to commend you for hiring such honest employees. I was at the dealer's service department last Saturday to have my shocks tested, and I was thrilled with the terrific service there. Although I had no appointment and had to wait for an hour for a mechanic to examine my car, his efforts to treat me with courtesy and fairness more than made up for the inconvenience.

Tom, the mechanic, was extremely helpful and honest about the work necessary on my car. He carefully explained the testing he planned to do, the results of his tests, and corrective action he planned to take. I had gone to Saturn expecting to be charged a great deal of money for the work. But Tom discovered the problem and the solution to be far less drastic than we both had originally anticipated. Because of his honesty, I saved several hundred dollars and a great deal of frustration.

I hope that you will extend my thanks to him. And please pass this information on to your supervisor. I want her to know that Tom is the reason that I will be coming back to the Saturn dealership for future repairs as they are needed.

I have owned my Saturn SL1 for several years now. I rarely have problems with it, but when I do, I dread taking it to mechanics. It seems as though they are all so untrustworthy. But my interaction with Tom has definitely changed that previously unhappy perception.

Warmest regards,

COMPLAINTS

• ABOUT DELIVERY OF NEWSPAPER •

Dear Mr. Alloy,

Two months ago I bought a subscription to the *Dallas Morning News* when I was solicited by phone. Although I have received an invoice for my order, I have yet to see a single newspaper. The salesperson had promised that I would begin receiving my papers immediately.

Would you please do one of the following: either ensure that delivery begins immediately or cancel my subscription and notify me of that cancellation?

I ordered the Sunday-only subscription for the special rate of $50 on January 7 when I spoke with Sheila. Enclosed is a copy of the invoice received on February 2. Naturally, I will not pay it until I begin receiving a paper.

Thank you for your attention to this matter.

Sincerely,

• ABOUT RESTAURANT OR FOOD SERVICE •

Dear Peggy:

Two evenings ago, I was in the MiShack's restaurant on Lovers Lane in Bedrock, and I received exceptionally poor service. It was obvious that the waitress and several others we observed working that night were incapable of keeping up with their customers' requests. The kitchen too was apparently overburdened. What other explanation could there be for the inadequacies that we experienced that evening?

I inform you of this because I suspect that it is not the first complaint you've received from your customers lately; so perhaps you will see your way to do something to rectify the problem. The waitress did inform us that the restaurant was understaffed that night. If this indeed was the case, then the problem and the solution belong to the management team.

Upon arrival, we had to wait 20 minutes to be seated. Such a wait is not so unusual for a busy restaurant on the weekend. I mention it only to establish that I do not expect miracles when a restaurant is so busy. However, I do expect that, once I am seated, the drinks arrive promptly. They did not. I expect the food order to be taken in a timely manner. It was not. And I expect the food, especially after having waited for so long for it to arrive, to be acceptable. It was not. It was cold, and the portions were much smaller than we are accustomed to receiving at MiShack's.

No matter how good employees are at their jobs, if they have too much to handle, they will perform poorly. I have been a MiShack's patron for a number of years, but if this sort of problem is going to persist, I will be forced to dine elsewhere.

Sincerely,

ORDERS AND CANCELLATIONS

• PLACING ORDER •

Dear Vita-Rite:

I saw your ad in *Healthy Times* and would like to order a 6-month supply of Vita-Rite's Detoxification Teas. The ad lists the discounted price at $24.99 (shipping charges included).

I am enclosing a check for the full amount. As I understand it, North Carolina residents don't need to add any sales tax. If that information is incorrect, perhaps I could be billed for the remaining few dollars after delivery. Please send my order to the address above.

Do you offer additional nutritional products? If you have a catalog, please send that along also.

Thank you,

• Checking Status of Order •

Dear Ms. Ross,

Last March I was at the Cultural Expo, where I bought a book from your booth. I also ordered a companion workbook two and a half months ago and have never received it. I have enjoyed the book so far, but I think it would be even more helpful, as is mentioned at the end of each chapter, if I could do the workbook exercises that accompany each section.

Would you please check on that order for me?

The title of the book is *Teach Yourself Spanish* by Skip and Maggie Garafulic. The name of the workbook is *Teach Yourself Spanish: Student Handbook of Exercises and Sample Tests*.

Enclosed is a copy of my receipt for both books. The shipping address in my letterhead is still current.

Thank you,

• RECEIVING DUPLICATE BILLING •

RE: Account 5555-5555-5555-5555

Dear Customer Service Representative:

I have just received a bill from Ranger Credit Card Company; it is the same bill that I received and paid last month.

The original bill was received on April 27, and the payment was mailed by regular mail on April 30. Please credit my account with that payment and deduct the interest and late-payment fee incorrectly charged this month.

A copy of my canceled check and also copies of both bills are enclosed.

Thank you,

• Canceling Order •

RE: Order 5895858

Dear Customer Service Representative:

Please cancel my order for the two suits and a pair of shoes (dated September 18). You recently notified me that the clothes were on back order and that you could not guarantee shipment until November. Because I need the clothes for a trip in October, neither outfit will be of use to me.

Please credit my account for the total amount ($413.56) immediately.

Thank you for the prompt notification that the suits are out of stock. That notice will give me enough time to order something else.

Sincerely,

• CANCELING UNSATISFACTORY SERVICE •

RE: Account 95455

Dear Mr. Tully:

Please cancel my weekly housecleaning service, effective immediately. I have phoned several times in the past year about the poor service that I've received from Metro-Maid, but I've not seen any improvement in the services. My previous calls have focused on the following recurring problems with your workers:

- Failure to bring their own cleaning supplies with them on occasion
- Carpets left unvacuumed behind doors and under movable furniture
- Glass surfaces left streaked and smeared
- Failure to stay the agreed-upon 3 hours to finish cleaning tasks

Please be sure to notify the team that usually cleans my house. In the past, they have shown up at the regular time—even though I had canceled the service for that week. This time, I am giving a full week's written notice so I will not be liable for any charges should the cleaning team fail to receive this message.

Sincerely,

• RETURNING DAMAGED PRODUCT •

RE: Invoice 4344436

Dear Customer Service Representative:

I ordered the matching Crystal Seaview paperweights on May 24 and received them damaged on June 26. Both are visibly cracked.

I am returning them to you via UPS. Please reimburse me for the full amount of postage, and send me replacement paperweights immediately.

These paperweights are a birthday gift for my business partner. Although I ordered them in plenty of time, the delay in having to wait for undamaged ones will certainly create a short deadline. Do you pay for shipping them overnight in such cases where the error is yours? I must have them by May 10.

Enclosed is the return order form and a copy of the UPS receipt.

Thank you,

• REQUESTING REFUND FOR DEFECTIVE PRODUCT OR POOR SERVICE •

RE: Invoice 49494

Dear Customer Service Agent:

I am returning my Compton Color Printer to you for an immediate refund. It has not worked properly since the day we purchased it, and we no longer have the inclination to wait for you to send other technicians to "adjust" it.

Please refund me in the full amount ($432.13), plus the shipping charges ($25.95) incurred when sending it back to you (shipping bill and original receipt enclosed).

The printer smears and smudges almost any document that it prints out, even those done only in black and white. The repairman that you sent out to examine it told us that he could find nothing wrong with the machine; he stated that the quality of the printed documents was simply the best we could expect from such a printer. Assuming that his diagnosis of the situation is true, we will be looking for a higher-quality printer that better meets our printing needs.

Sincerely,

• REQUESTING REPLACEMENT UNDER WARRANTY •

RE: Invoice 00012

Dear Mrs. Blakely:

I bought a vegetable steamer/rice cooker about 6 months ago at Mincefield's Department Store (Model 120-V, with a 1-year warranty). When I tried to use it last week, however, the power button would not work. I returned the item to the store, but Mincefield's would not honor the guarantee, because it is going out of business. The manager suggested that I contact you, the manufacturer.

I need to have the steamer either repaired or replaced. Also, I assume that I will be reimbursed for shipping charges, so I'm enclosing the post office receipt with this letter. Please return the new or repaired steamer to my work address: 2003 Mountainview, Suite 320, Houston, TX 79050.

I use the steamer/cooker quite frequently so I would appreciate your promptness. Except for the fact that it suddenly broke last week, I find it extremely convenient, a product well worth buying.

Thank you for honoring the manufacturer's warranty. I'll look forward to purchasing other of your products.

Thank you,

REQUESTS

• REMOVING NAME FROM MAILING LIST •

RE: Account 686869566

Dear Customer Service Agent:

I recently became a new MasterWorld credit card member. From the time that I received my first statement, I have been inundated with a never-ending stream of advertisements and mail-order offers through, I suppose, this credit card mailing list. I do not like to shop by mail and simply discard my "junk mail."

I would be much more satisfied with my credit card services if you would please remove my name from your mailing list. The only mail that I wish to receive from your organization is my monthly billing statement.

Thank you for removing my name from your direct-mail marketing lists and refusing to sell it to other companies.

Sincerely,

• REQUESTING RETURN OF DEPOSIT •

Dear Apartment Manager,

Last month I placed a deposit on an apartment in your complex. The representative with whom I spoke promised me at that time that I would be able to move into my new apartment within 2 weeks. It has now been 4 weeks and the apartment still isn't ready for me.

The lease on my old apartment expired a week ago, so I was forced to find other accommodations in another apartment complex. Since I am now leasing from them, I am requesting that you send me a full refund of the deposit I made to you a month ago.

Please send the check to my new address at 22 Bluebonnet Lane, #221, Dalworthington MD 39473. Or you may contact me by phone (555-5555) and I will pick the check up personally.

Thank you,

• NOTIFYING COMPANY OF HAZARDOUS PRODUCT •

Dear Mr. Saltillo,

A few weeks ago I bought a decorative bowl manufactured by your company. Although it makes a beautiful centerpiece, I noticed on the enclosed information leaflet that the bowl contains lead.

Knowing how dangerous lead poisoning is and how easy it is to get lead poisoning from food served in a lead dish, I think it's important that you warn customers. I suggest that you use bold print on the outside of the box. Clarify that the notice of lead content is a warning, not just a characteristic of the clay.

The bowl I now own is the size C serving bowl from the Printemps collection. I have enclosed my proof of purchase here as well as a copy of the leaflet that came with the dish.

I think that many customers are unaware of the danger of lead poisoning. Please do everything that you can to see that unnecessary poisoning does not occur.

Sincerely,

CREDIT, BANKING, AND FINANCIAL CONCERNS

Nothing captures the attention of readers so much as the issue of money—their money or yours. Whether depositing, withdrawing, lending, or borrowing, you want to make sure you provide all the facts.

When you have borrowed money, assure the reader that you intend to repay the money owed, even if that becomes necessary under altered terms with lesser amounts or over a longer period. Although many people consider their financial situation confidential, you will do well to explain your current difficulties to those who are lending you money. They consider explanations a show of good faith. Another way to motivate creditors to work with you during difficult times is to remind them about past business you've given them and state your intention to do business with them again under better conditions.

When requesting a loan, give a full explanation of how you intend to use the money and state your plans for repayment. Be specific as to your calculations for where the money will come from to repay the loan. Even when addressing friends or family, use a businesslike (not flippant or pleading) tone to convey your sincere need for the money and your firm intention to repay the loan.

When refusing a loan to friend, remember that you are not obligated to give a reason—although doing so makes your refusal sound less arbitrary and more thoughtful. Statements such as these may seem firm, yet less harsh.

"I feel uncomfortable making personal loans for any reason to anyone."

"I'm not financially in a position to make loans to anyone."

"My spouse and I have made a personal commitment to each other never to lend money to a friend or a relative because of the hard feelings that inevitably develop around such circumstances."

"My own job is rather unstable."

When refusing a loan, however, do express your understanding of the need for the money. Often, when the requester hears a "no," he or she thinks that you are saying no simply because you don't earnestly see the need as critical or urgent. Consider these comments:

"I understand how much you need the money."

"I can understand the difficulty of the situation."

"You have cause for concern. I see your predicament."

"A couple of thousand dollars, I know, would make a big difference in your situation. I understand that."

Try to use positive phrasing with your turndown:

"I'm afraid I simply can't make such a loan. I need all my available resources to handle my own commitments."

"I wish I could help in this incident, but I can't."

"I wish I had the extra money for situations like this, but I just don't. We live on a limited income ourselves."

Instead of focusing on what you're not going to provide, focus on your own needs or plans for the money or your own positive philosophies about personal loans.

"I myself have similar commitments that will require all my available cash. We plan to spend any excess cash above our expenses this year on X."

End with a goodwill statement about the outcome of the situation or resolution of any problem.

"I do hope you can resolve the issue."

"I'll hope to hear that you've been able to handle the situation on your own."

"I hope you'll understand. I do value our relationship and want what is best for both of us."

In delicate matters such as lending, borrowing, and collecting, tone becomes very important in reaffirming commitments and in keeping any personal relationship intact.

On other miscellaneous matters of banking, finance, and taxes, summarize your message succinctly without irrelevant detail: What do you want your reader to know or do? Include all necessary dates, account numbers, amounts, full names, and form or receipt numbers so the reader can investigate your history and situation with ease. The image that you create in your writing style and with your thoroughness often makes an impression that spills over into the business transaction and decision itself.

If you decide to grant a loan, state your positive response immediately.

"I'm enclosing the money asked for."

"Yes, we will agree to lend you the money under the terms you mentioned."

"We are glad to be able to help you out in this incidence."

Outline the conditions under which you will make the loan, including all repayment terms and any collateral you expect.

"We understand that you intend to begin repaying the money in June."

"I can agree to the 10 percent interest over the term of the loan."

"The details you outlined for repayment dates and amounts sound fine."

Provide a written agreement of the loan and repayment schedule for the friend or family member to sign. This formality underscores your own firm intention that the borrower will repay the loan by the agreed-upon date. This agreement also offers protection in case the borrower dies; you'll need proof of the money owed to you from the deceased's estate.

> *"I've drafted a letter, including the details of the loan."*
>
> *"I've put together a confirmation of the loan and terms."*
>
> *"Just so we both understand the terms of the loan, I've outlined here something for you to sign so that both of us are clear about the situation."*
>
> *"In case something happens to me or you before this loan is repaid, I've jotted down the particulars…"*

CREDIT AND COLLECTIONS

• ADDING PERSON TO ACCOUNT •

RE: Checking Account 099090933

Dear Mr. Osorio:

I have recently married and would like to add my husband to my checking account.

An account manager at Corporate Bank told me last week that my husband and his bank (Service Corp. United) must complete a few forms for an electronic transfer of his account balance to your bank. Please send me those forms immediately so that we can take care of this transfer before we leave town on April 30.

Thank you. We're looking forward to continued excellent service at your bank.

Sincerely,

• REMOVING PERSON FROM ACCOUNT •

RE: Checking Account 3434898755534

Dear Customer Service Representative:

My mother and I have been cosignatories on the same checking account since 1995. She is now moving to Florida, so she plans to open a separate account there in her name only.

Please take the necessary steps to remove her name from our joint account. Any paperwork to be completed may be sent to me at the address on the letterhead.

My mother plans to move within the next 3 weeks, so we'll appreciate your making this change promptly.

Thank you,

(Signatures of both parties)

• NOTIFYING OF PAYMENT NOT CREDITED TO ACCOUNT •

RE: Service Card Account 7878-9033-9933

Dear Ms. Garcia:

Three weeks ago, on November 20, I sent a payment of $200 to the Service Card. However, when I received my last billing statement, dated November 30, that payment had still not been credited. What is more, I was charged a $15 late fee for failure to pay.

Would you please verify your receipt of that payment and see that I am credited in the full amount? Once the first discrepancy is remedied, please subtract the $15 late fee erroneously added to my balance.

I mailed the payment 10 days before the due date (as I usually do), so the Service Card should have received my check in plenty of time to apply the payment before the closing date for November's statement.

Enclosed is a copy of my check carbon, on which is imprinted the check that I wrote to the Service Card 3 weeks ago.

Sincerely,

• **REQUESTING RECONSIDERATION FOR DENIED CHARGE ACCOUNT** •

Dear New Accounts:

I received your notice that I was denied a personal charge account with your department store. I cannot understand this refusal of credit, because my credit history is exemplary.

The income from my salary and my husband's business totals $52,000. Perhaps you considered us a credit risk because his income is from self-employment and I've just begun my new job this month. Yes, I have recently changed jobs, but you'll notice that I was with my previous employer for more than 7 years. As to my husband's income from his small business, I'm enclosing his corporate tax returns for the past 2 years to substantiate his average income at $31,000.

We respectfully ask that you reconsider your decision regarding our credit status. I'd be happy to resubmit the application to ensure that no discrepancies exist. Or, if you must adhere to your decision, please notify me (my address and phone number are on the letterhead) of the reasons that led to your decision.

I submitted my application to you on March 19, and your response (enclosed) is dated March 31. We hope to hear from you promptly with a more positive answer so that we can begin to do business with your fine department store.

Sincerely,

• CLAIMING BANKRUPTCY PROTECTION •

Dear Capital Bank:

Please discontinue immediately your calls and letters demanding payment. You were notified that I filed bankruptcy in Atlanta, Georgia, on February 1, 19—, under Docket number 499993433872983459595. (Enclosed is another such copy of that action.)

As you may be aware, all creditors, once they have been notified of such action, are subject to stiff penalties and fines should they persist in collecting their debts directly or through a second party.

If you have further questions about the bankruptcy proceedings, you may contact my lawyer: Ms. Sheila Burnett, 4885 Westlake, Ste 344, Atlanta, Georgia.

Yours truly,

• DOCUMENTING LOST OR STOLEN CREDIT CARD •

RE: Stolen card 456-999-30303

Dear Credit Services:

One week ago (September 16) I noticed that my credit card had been lost, and I immediately called to report it. Now I'm following up that report with a letter for your records.

If you have not already done so, please take the necessary actions to change my account numbers and discontinue the old card. Also, please send my new card as soon as possible.

According to your credit card contract, I will not be responsible for any authorized charges above $50 resulting from this lost card and my subsequent report.

For your convenience, I am enclosing a copy of the last statement from Capital Credit. The only missing information is my full name as printed on the card (Pasquel R. Venet) and my current address: 2102 Rue-de-Calais, Pendleton, MO 87726.

Thank you,

• REQUESTING CREDIT REPORT •

Dear Credit Bureau:

I would like to request a personal credit report. Please send the report to the current address listed below.

The necessary personal information is as follows:

- Social security number: 555-55-5555
- Date of birth: February 24, 1968
- Current address: 14300 Oak Tree Lane, #21A, Mobile, AL 39957 (I have lived at this address since December 1996.)
- Prior address: 1520 Maple Avenue, #917, Mobile, AL 39902. (I lived at that address for 4 years, from January 1992 to December 1996.)
- Name change: Maiden name (Collins) legally changed to Banderas in April 1995.

I understand that you need address information going back only 5 years. If this requirement has changed, please notify me immediately so I can include more information.

Also, enclosed is a copy of my driver's license to verify my current address. Because it still shows my maiden name, I have enclosed a copy of my marriage certificate as well.

Sincerely,

• DISPUTING CREDIT REPORT •

RE: Social Security Number 455-90-9000

Dear Mr. Hirschowitz:

The mortgage loan that I applied for on October 12 was denied on the basis of information supplied by your credit bureau. The erroneous information contained in your credit bureau's report involved "late payments" on my car for 36 months. I assure you that I made those payments on time.

Please contact Ford Motor Company to verify that this is fact, and correct my credit report with your bureau. Then please send me a new, corrected credit report at the above address.

I have already been in touch with Ford Motor Company and received an explanation of the mix-up on the car payments. When I bought my car, I made the first 2-months' payments immediately. For some reason, however, the first payment was credited as two January payments instead of one January and one February payment. So when I made no payment the next month (for February), my record was marked as "late." From that point on, all my payments were logged as a month behind, even though I was paying them on time.

I am enclosing a copy of the credit bureau report you supplied to the mortgage company, containing the erroneous information. Also included is a printout of my Ford Motor Company record of payments, and a business card from Susan Richards (the Ford customer service agent who supplied me with the printout). She will be happy to speak with you regarding this issue.

Sincerely,

BANKING

• OPENING ACCOUNT •

Dear Mr. Manion:

I would like to open a personal checking account. Because it is difficult for me to find the time to come in during business hours, I would like to handle the transaction entirely by mail.

Please send me the proper signature forms to be filled out, as well as any pertinent information you may have for me with regard to bank policies and regulations.

I need a checking account with unlimited checking privileges and would like to avoid monthly service charges by maintaining your minimum balance requirements. As to my choice of checks, please select a style comparable to the sample I'm enclosing from my current account with another bank. As you open the account, please order the minimum number of checks (that is usually 200 checks, I think) and debit my account for that cost.

My current address is 2410 Lakebetter Court, Oklahoma City, OK 83432. If you need any additional information in order to send the signature forms and open the account, please call me at my daytime work number (555-5555). Your bank has an excellent reputation in the community, and I'm looking forward to a solid banking relationship.

Sincerely,

• CLOSING ACCOUNT •

Because of Better Rates

RE: Joint Checking Account 89983334555

Dear Mr. Pfaff:

I am closing my account with First United Bank and moving my account to my credit union because of the convenience involved.

Would you please send a final statement and a cashier's check for the closing balance of $1249, according to my records, to the address above?

The service at First United has always been fine, but a credit union better serves my needs at the present time. In fact, its savings accounts offer much better interest rates than your bank does.

Please note both my wife's and my notarized signatures below.

Sincerely,

• CLOSING ACCOUNT •

Because of Moving

RE: Checking Account 9883440003

Dear Mr. Davila:

I have a regular checking account with Eagle Bend Bank, and I am moving to New York City next week. Because Eagle Bend doesn't have a branch there, I must close my account here and build a new banking relationship in New York.

Please send me the latest statement and any other information that I may need to close the account. I don't plan to write any more checks on the account, and I want a chance to review your records before I close the account and accept the final balance as accurate.

I leave Eagle Bend on Thursday, March 31. That is only 9 days away, so I'd be grateful for your expediency in sending the paperwork.

Thank you,

• CLOSING ACCOUNT •

Because of Poor Service

Dear Account Manager,

I have had both checking and savings accounts with Bank of Trust since 1993, but I'm closing both of my accounts today. Why? I can no longer tolerate the poor service that I've been receiving the past year.

When I phoned the bank on Monday, account manager Stephanie Maxwell informed me that a letter of intent is all that is required to close my accounts. Please make the necessary arrangements to properly close my accounts with Bank of Trust.

Over the last year, I have been subject to a number of accounting errors on the part of Bank of Trust. On more than one occasion, for example, I was charged for overdrafts that occurred because of a teller's error. (Notice my August, October, and November statements for those improper charges.) Mistakes happen, but my attempts to have the problems redressed were most often met with more bureaucracy, incompetence, and even rudeness.

I am enclosing copies of my last bank statement and my last savings account summary for your convenience in closing the accounts.

Yours truly,

• DISPUTING ACCOUNT STATEMENT •

Service Charge

RE: Checking Account 987654321

Dear Ms. Sirikul:

On my last checking account statement, I noticed that I was charged for calling the Certified Bank automated teller information number. I have been using that number (toll-free) to verify deposits and withdrawals for years (ever since I opened my account in 1992) and was unaware of any new policy about charges for using that number.

If indeed some new policy imposes a charge for its use, I will no longer call that number. In any case, I think it only fair that you credit my account for the $7 charge for the seven times that I called the number during my last banking cycle.

If there was a policy change imposing that new usage fee, notification prior to the start of the new policy was in order. I never received such notice and, therefore, do not expect to be charged for a service that I have been receiving free for so long.

Enclosed is a copy of my last statement with the extra service charges highlighted in yellow. I will appreciate your removing these charges.

Sincerely,

• DISPUTING ACCOUNT STATEMENT •

Failure to Credit Deposit

RE: Checking Account 34889893483

Dear Mrs. Skidmore,

One week ago, on November 22, I deposited $637.12 in my regular checking account through your automated teller. However, the deposit has not yet been credited to my account.

Please verify that deposit and call me immediately (456-0004) if there some problem.

It is my understanding that a deposit is always credited the day it is made (or the following business day if it is made after 3 p.m.). If this policy has changed, please notify me at once. Otherwise, I will assume that it remains the same and will continue to do my banking accordingly.

I am enclosing a copy of the deposit slip to help you track the deposit.

Sincerely,

• DISPUTING ACCOUNT STATEMENT •

Insufficient Funds

RE: Checking Account 00939399087675

Dear Ms. Aurilia:

I just received a notice of insufficient funds from Interstate Bank. The notice states that a standard $20 service charge has been assessed to my account to cover administration fees involving a returned check. I have double-checked my records and verified that I made a deposit on August 6 that was not credited to my account until August 8. Therefore, check 2223 to Doyen's Department Store was returned through no fault of my own.

Please double-check your records, and correct the date of the deposit in question. Then please credit back to my account the $20 service charge for the overdraft. Finally, as you are aware, there is embarrassment in having a check returned marked "insufficient funds." I'd appreciate it if you would notify the department store that the error was the bank's, not mine.

As you will see on the deposit slip enclosed with this letter, I made the deposit before 3 p.m. on the same day that the check was cashed (June 22). There should have been more than enough money in my account to cover the check.

Thank you for your attention in correcting this error promptly.

Sincerely,

Enc. Your notification of insufficient funds

• REQUESTING LOAN •

Dear Mrs. L'Argent:

I am in the process of paying off a number of small debts. In an effort to simplify my finances, reduce the aggregate interest that I am charged every month, and reduce the total of my overall monthly payments, I would like to acquire a consolidation loan.

Please review the enclosed loan proposal. I am seeking approval by the end of this week, if at all possible, before I incur additional interest charges on my various debts.

The loans that I would like to consolidate include four credit cards (two majors and two department stores), my remaining six car payments, a furniture store credit plan, and a few small payments for dental work last year. Other details and numbers are, of course, included in the loan proposal. As collateral for the loan, I'm suggesting my 1997 Cherokee Jeep and my wife's 1997 Buick.

My total annual income amounts to $43,550. That income should certainly be sufficient to pay off the loan. My past financial problems have been the result of a 6-month period of unemployment. Now that I've found a new job, I find that I'm still "playing catch-up" with the bills. Until this past difficulty, my credit rating was fine and with this consolidation loan, I'm hoping to regain my footing and establish consistent payment patterns.

My net worth calculations (assets and liabilities) are contained on the completed form supplied by your customer service representative. Thank you for your consideration.

Sincerely,

• REQUESTING EXPLANATION OF LOAN DENIAL •

Dear Loan Officer:

Your bank recently denied my request for a $4000 personal improvement loan. I am puzzled by your decision and respectfully request an explanation for refusing the loan.

I have been steadily employed with the same company for the past 3 years, earning $32,000 annually. I have always paid my bills on time and have an excellent credit rating.

What other possible risk factor could your loan committee be considering? If its decision was based on some erroneous report by a credit agency, I'd like to be made aware of that so I can correct any discrepancies immediately.

Was there some other error or reason? What will be necessary for you to reconsider my loan application? I'll look forward to either an explanation or a positive decision upon a second analysis.

Sincerely,

• REQUESTING LOAN PAYMENT ADJUSTMENT •

RE: Loan 585857

Dear Loan Officer:

My spouse was recently laid off from his job, and we are having difficulty meeting our financial obligations during this interim period while he seeks other employment.

We are asking that you defer or reduce our $425 monthly loan payments until he finds other employment. If you cannot defer payments completely for a few months, we believe that we can continue to make payments of about $100 each month until our employment situation improves.

My job is steady, and we intend to pay the loan in full as soon as possible. I'm enclosing a $100 payment in good faith, hoping you will agree to this reduced-payment arrangement, if not a complete deferral.

When conditions improve for us, we will look forward to continuing our banking relationship with your organization in future years. Thank you for your understanding and patience in this difficult time.

Sincerely,

• REQUESTING DEFERRED PAYMENT ON LOAN •

RE: Loan 88844

Dear Loan Officer:

My car loan payment falls due on the seventh of the month, and I'm requesting that you change the payment due date to the first of the month. I travel frequently on my job and therefore try to write all my checks twice a month. The current due date creates either the inconvenience of having to mail the payment from the road or the necessity of making the payment early.

I'll appreciate your changing the monthly due date and am willing to make any partial payment necessary to cover the interest on the interim days during the changeover.

Sincerely,

• CASHING CERTIFICATE OF DEPOSIT •

RE: Certificate of Deposit 3239995

Dear Customer Service Representative:

The above certificate of deposit for $10,000 will mature on November 1, and I intend to cash the CD on that date. Would you please deposit the full value at maturity in my personal checking account 4949477002, also at your institution?

Sincerely,

• CHECKING STATUS OF INVESTMENT ACCOUNT •

RE: Heritage Mutual Fund Account 4958882

Dear Fund Agent:

Would you please forward a current statement of my investment account to the above address? I'd also like a summary explanation of the performance of my investments with your fund since my initial deposit of $4560 on January 10, 1997.

As a means to analyzing my overall return, would you please provide any further information, analysis, ratings, or comparisons with other funds sharing the same investment objectives?

Also, it would be helpful to know if investment philosophies will change now that you have a new fund manager.

Sincerely,

• DOCUMENTING LOSS OF SAFETY DEPOSIT BOX KEY •

RE: Safety Deposit Box 59995

Dear Customer Service Representative:

I have either misplaced or lost the key to my safety deposit box. This letter is being sent to follow up my telephone report of the lost key on May 2.

Please make your staff aware of any possible attempts at unauthorized use in case someone has stolen or found the key. The last time I entered the box was almost 5 months ago, in early January. Could you please check your records and let me know if there has been any unauthorized activity on the box in this intervening time? If so, I'll appreciate your sending me a copy of the transaction/entry dates, names, and signatures.

Finally, would you please assign me a new box? If you will phone me when it's ready, I'll stop by to complete the necessary signature form. I appreciate your effort on my behalf to ensure safekeeping of my valuables.

Sincerely,

TAXES

• REQUESTING EXTENSION FOR FILING RETURN •

RE: Social Security Number 123-45-6789
   Tax Year 19—

Dear IRS Representative:

With this letter, I am requesting a second extension on filing my income tax return for this past year. I filed Form 4868 for the first extension on April 1, along with my payment of $450 for additional taxes.

This second extension has become necessary because my job has required that I unexpectedly be out of the country for an extended period (November 1996 to the present). When I left the United States in November, I had no idea that my stay here in the Philippines would be extended on a month-by-month basis. Because of the delay in forwarding information overseas, I am having difficulty collecting all my 1099s and other financial reports from various investment accounts.

Also, my CPA tax preparer from past years has retired, and I'm trying to select a new one to prepare this year's return. The process of interviewing CPAs by letter and checking references with their long-time customers has become complicated and time-consuming because of my overseas work.

For both of these reasons, I'm requesting an additional extension of the filing deadline. Would you please confirm this extension by writing to me at the above address?

Sincerely,

• DISPUTING REFUND RECEIVED •

RE: Social Security Number 123-45-6789

I have just received my refund check for $3488 on my 19—return, $1500 less than the amount due me according to my records and the submitted return.

Your attached letter explained that you had discovered unreported earnings from royalties of $6000 on a 1099 submitted by my publisher. However, those royalty earnings *have been reported*.

That royalty amount was reported on my business return rather than my personal return for this past year. All personal royalties go into my business account. If you'll cross-reference my corporate tax return for Trudeau and Associates, you'll notice that these earnings have been reported in that income total.

Therefore, please correct your records and forward to me the remainder of my refund, $1500, along with the accrued interest to date. Thank you.

Yours truly,

• RESPONDING TO AUDIT OR CLARIFICATION OF RETURN •

RE: Social Security Number 123-45-6789
  Audit Number 34999333399393
  Tax Year 19—

Dear IRS Representative:

In response to your notification that my 19— federal tax return is being audited, I am enclosing the following items you requested to support my charitable contributions deduction:

- My contribution record to my church
- Receipts for items donated to Goodwill Industries
- Transactions receipts for stock sold and contributed to Star Hope Mission

These receipts and contribution records should answer your questions about the return. If not, please phone me at (344) 499-4444 (daytime) or (443) 666-0909 (evening).

Yours truly,

• REQUESTING REVIEW •

RE: Social Security Number 123-45-6789
Audit Number 94949491223
Tax Year 19—

Dear IRS Representative:

The auditors have completed their review of my 19— income tax return. They have assessed my tax liabilities at $13,478 rather than the claimed $8232, calculated by my own CPA tax preparer.

I disagree with your auditors' conclusions and the additional proposed tax liability. The auditors have questioned my charitable contribution of an unimproved lot to the First United Methodist Church. Although churches do not assess a value to the property they receive but rather simply acknowledge receipt, I secured and submitted two appraisals from independent appraisal companies attesting to the value of the land. The appraisal estimates were within $1000 of each other. Although the IRS auditors consider the value to be excessive for an unimproved lot, its prime location as a parking lot for surrounding businesses is the basis for those appraised values.

Granted, the appraisal value shown by the Barrington Independent School District is $15,000 less than that assessed by the appraisers, but all properties in the district have been undervalued. A recent newspaper article states that property owners can expect all tax assessments to rise by 30 to 50 percent in the next 2 years. (Copies of that article and the two appraisals from the independent appraisal companies are enclosed.)

Therefore, with this letter, I'm requesting an independent review of my tax return and the examination findings by the Appeals Office.

My daytime phone number is (477) 555-7878. Thank you for your prompt review.

Yours truly,

Enc. Auditing findings and IRS letter
　　　Two appraisals on land
　　　Newspaper article about appraisals

• DISPUTING PROPERTY TAX ASSESSMENT •

County Tax Assessor

RE: Lot 789879
     Block 37B
     Index Number 8999833

Dear Tax Assessor:

The recent tax assessment on my lot on Hughes Road seems excessive. The current assessment of $4888 represents a 48 percent increase over the amount assessed last year on the property.

I realize that almost all property taxes were increased this past year, but the assessment is far greater than that for the lots surrounding the property. The lot to the left was assessed at $3600; the lot to the right was assessed at $3598; the lot across the street was appraised at $3489. These are all comparable investment lots, with no improvements on them. None is a corner lot, and none has utilities.

I can imagine only that someone made a clerical error in computing the assessment. Would you please review this situation and respond to me at my home address (124 Zimmer Avenue) immediately about this assessment? If I do not hear from you within 2 weeks, I will plan to appeal the assessment to the State Board of Review.

Sincerely,

INSURANCE

• REQUESTING INFORMATION ON INSURANCE COMPANY •

Dear Insurance Commissioner:

I would like information on the Universal Insurance Company before I make a decision about applying for coverage.

Specifically, I would appreciate answers to the following questions:

- Is the company licensed to operate in our state?
- How is the company rated by the industry?
- Is the company financially stable? Are there any bankruptcy proceedings in the past or in progress?
- Have you received any complaints about the company or its representatives with regard to the way they have represented themselves, paid claims to policyholders, misrepresented their services, or failed to provide adequate customer service?

One of Universal's direct-mail pieces came to my home recently, advertising an annual premium for health coverage that seems quite low and that triggered both my interest and my doubt. Any information you can provide will be most helpful to me in making my decision about talking with the company representative further about coverage. Thank you for your assistance.

Sincerely,

• CONVERTING COMPANY POLICY TO INDIVIDUAL POLICY •

Dear Insurance Representative:

I currently have life and medical insurance coverage with your company through my employer, McDonnelly-Dudley, Inc., policy number WTYl345. Effective May 1, I will be leaving this company and am considering my option to convert my group coverage to an individual policy.

Would you please provide me with an overview of the procedure to make this conversion within the next 30 days? I also need information about coverage and costs: the monthly premiums for various amounts of coverage, any deductibles involved, and any health maintenance services or discounts.

I am married, with one child. For the purpose of computing our premiums, our birthdays follow:

> John C. Fairchild: 1/30/52
> Marcia Bowen Fairchild: 2/26/54
> Gerald Fairchild: 7/1/84

Although I have not accepted a new position with another employer, I do not anticipate my occupational duties to change significantly, and, therefore should pose no additional insurance risks.

I'll appreciate your fast response with this information because I must convert to an individual policy by May 31.

Sincerely,

• CHANGING LIFE INSURANCE BENEFICIARY •

RE: Term Life Insurance Policy 4449099

Dear Insurance Agent:

I want to change the beneficiary on my term life insurance policy, effective immediately. The current beneficiary is Albert P. Gunn (husband). I'd like the new beneficiaries to be my parents: Marcus and Louise Hayward. All other provisions and clauses of the policy will remain the same.

I am enclosing my notarized signature below. Should there be other forms required, please send those immediately to my work address: 3499 Beltway Drive, Suite 395, Dallas, TX 75252. Thank you.

Sincerely,

• REQUESTING NEW AGENT—POOR SERVICE •

RE: Homeowner's Policy RT3889

Dear Manager:

My current insurance agent (Ken Blackman of Ardmore, Oklahoma) has not been as attentive as necessary to my insurance coverage in the past, and I am requesting that a new agent service my account. Would you please have a new agent (preferably one a little closer to my current location) contact me immediately?

I've been a policyholder for more than 10 years and think that some additional coverage is warranted because of various jewelry and computer purchases through the years. My current agent has never mentioned updating my coverage. Additionally, I recently had a small claim (broken picture window) and found it difficult to get Mr. Blackman to return my calls.

Please let me know if any further action is required on my part, and I'll look forward to having a new agent from your organization contact me about taking over the account.

Sincerely,

• REQUESTING REDUCTION OF HEALTH INSURANCE PREMIUM •

RE: Medical Insurance Policy 5899985

Dear Insurance Agent:

I am requesting a reassessment of the risk associated with the premiums on my current insurance policy, issued 8 years ago.

A recent physical exam shows that I am now within the standard weight guidelines; also, I am no longer a smoker. With these improvements to my lifestyle, my doctor agrees that my health risks have decreased. (His letter is attached.)

Would you please let me know if I now qualify for lower rates, and send me any necessary forms and verification of the change in premium payments?

Sincerely,

• REQUESTING REDUCTION OF AUTO INSURANCE RATE •

RE: Auto Policy 58838

Dear Insurance Agent:

I've just received my new premium notice reflecting the addition of my son, Jeff Lassiter, age 16, to my auto policy, effective August 6. That increase in premium seems to be excessive for his limited use of my car.

Would you please reevaluate the risk factors associated with his driving and let us know what discounts you can offer in his case?

Jeff completed the state-approved safe-driving course this past spring at Lamar High School. As an honor student there, he has shown considerable maturity for his age and has never been involved in acts of delinquency or irresponsibility. His driving will be limited to trips to school and to church youth functions, all within a 10-mile radius of our home.

We'll look forward to a positive decision about reduced rates for responsible, limited driving by my son.

Sincerely,

• CLAIMING LIFE INSURANCE BENEFITS •

RE: Life Insurance Policy 44922

Dear Insurance Agent:

Randall O. Flemming, your policyholder, died on August 1 in Houston, Texas. His latest legal residence was 4788 Elmhurst in Houston. As beneficiary of his life insurance policy, I am requesting immediate settlement of the lump-sum distribution.

I would prefer to have electronic transfer of the funds direct to my bank account 0039884993 at BankFirst, Houston, TX 77013. If for some reason you are not set up to make an electronic transfer, you may mail the distribution check directly to me at the above address.

Enclosed is the required, signed certificate of death.

Sincerely,

• DISPUTING AMOUNT OF SETTLEMENT •

RE: Homeowner's Policy 5500003

Dear Claims Adjuster:

Today I received your letter and settlement check for replacement of my television sets, security system, and stereo equipment, which were damaged when lightning struck our home on March 6. That settlement amount is unacceptable.

Please review the attached documentation (original receipts for purchase of each item), which shows the total cost to be $9456. It seems that your settlement check is for $7092, representing a payment of 25 percent lower than actual value. I suppose this discounted replacement payment is based on a typical deduction for normal wear and tear.

From the dates on the receipts, you'll notice that all the equipment was new. In fact, we purchased our newly constructed home only 6 weeks ago. Although we closed on the home January 27, we took possession from the builder only 3 days before the lightning incident. (Our receipt for the move with Bekins, showing the move-in date as March 3, is enclosed.) Therefore, the damaged items were virtually unused. We believe that we are entitled to full replacement values under these circumstances.

We ask that you reevaluate our situation and send us another check for $2364 to bring the total settlement to the appropriate replacement amount of $9456.

Sincerely,

• CANCELING POLICY •

RE: Homeowner's Policy 778890
    Auto Policy 5588839
    Term Life Insurance Policy 488779

Dear Mr. Herman:

I would like to cancel all three of the above policies, effective May 31. Please return any portion of the premium payments due me under the 6-month payment plan for each.

Since applying for the life policy, I have discovered another policy that will meet my needs for coverage at better rates, and I plan to convert to whole life insurance with that new company.

Additionally, I have been disappointed with the way my homeowner's account has been serviced for the past 18 months. When I recently reported a claim for carpet damage due to a broken plumbing line, I had great difficulty in getting a quick estimate for repairs and replacement carpet installed through your designated vendor (M. C. McElrath Flooring).

And because of dissatisfaction with these two policies, I've simply decided to move all three of my insurance accounts to another company.

Thank you for your prompt processing of this cancellation notice and premium refund.

Sincerely,

• APPEALING POLICY TERMINATION TO COMPANY PRESIDENT •

RE: Homeowner's Policy 998822

Dear Mr. Windover:

I have been a policyholder with your company for the past 8 years and to date I've paid premiums totaling $9350. Yet, unexpectedly, I've received a notice from your company stating that you plan to cancel my homeowner's coverage, effective February 1. Certainly, there has been some mistake.

Would you please investigate the matter and let me know why this action is planned?

During the past 8 years, I've filed one claim for $4200 for roof damage after a hailstorm on May 18 of this year. Your claims adjuster investigated the roof damage, and I selected your recommended roofer for the repairs. There are no other extenuating circumstances of which I'm aware.

If after reviewing the situation, you decide not to reverse the decision and reinstate my coverage, I plan to cancel my other policies with your organization:

Policy 009898   Auto insurance, in effect for 10 years
Policy 899998   Auto insurance, in effect for 6 years
Policy 777888   Auto insurance (son, Michael Ray), in effect for 2 years

Additionally, I plan to contact the State Department of Insurance and ask for a review of this decision, fearing that other homeowners who were victims of hail damage in the same storm have received or will receive similar cancellation notices.

I'll look forward to your explanation about the homeowner's cancellation notice and hope that you can reverse that decision so that I can continue my coverage with your organization.

Sincerely,

• APPEALING POLICY TERMINATION TO REGULATORY AGENCY •

RE: Policy T388872
Wobbly Insurance Company
4889 Wimbledon Drive
Albany, NY 12207

Dear Mr. Breslin:

On October 15, my Cherokee Jeep was stolen from the airport parking lot. I filed a claim with the Wobbly Insurance Company according to the standard procedure. The settlement has been unacceptable, and I'm appealing to you to arbitrate the decision and review Wobbly's license to sell insurance in our state.

The company sent me a settlement check for $9400, nearly $2000 below the blue-book value of jeeps of the same year and comparable mileage and condition as mine. I wrote the company to protest its arbitrary decision, enclosing a copy of the blue-book page and a copy of an appraisal from a local dealership. Wobbly refused to increase the amount offered in its settlement.

Therefore, I'm appealing to you for your arbitration and will abide by your decision in this case. Additionally, I suggest that you review the company's standard procedures for paying other auto claims; in my dealing with Wobbly representatives, their cavalier attitude seems to indicate that such treatment is rather commonplace. I strongly urge you to revoke the company's license for selling insurance in New York.

Sincerely,

DECLINING INVITATIONS OR REQUESTS

Most people hate to say no—but not nearly as much as other people hate to hear it. Your challenge in declining invitations and solicitations, therefore, is to extricate yourself from the situation or obligation while maintaining the relationship or good standing.

To do so, state your empathetic understanding of the need, request, or situation. Often people assume that your "no" means that you do not thoroughly understand the real situation or need. You have to take care to demonstrate to readers that you do have an appreciation of the situation and their need for your services or money.

As a first step then, agree, if you can do so honestly, that the need is real or the cause is worthwhile.

"I understand that this need is real."

"I identify with your goals."

"I concur with the action you plan to take."

"The cause is certainly deserving of support and attention."

Add your reason for a negative response, if you wish. Giving a reason makes your decision sound less arbitrary and more thoughtful.

"I've simply overcommitted myself at this point."

"My schedule has just become too unpredictable."

"I've made previous commitments for the funds this year."

"I simply couldn't feel comfortable making that commitment, because other commitments for my time would have to go lacking."

165

Be firm about your decision not to contribute, participate, or attend. On occasion, you may find it easier to phrase a negative message positively by focusing on what you *do* intend to do with your time, money, or possessions rather than on what you can't do. Example:

"This year I plan to spend my time exclusively in helping the X Committee to…"

And by all means, end with a goodwill statement about the positive outcome for the event, occasion, situation, or cause.

"I wish you every success with the project."

"Thank you for thinking of me."

"I appreciate your letting me know of the efforts and goals of your group."

"I know you'll be outrageously successful with such an event."

"The party sounds like a wonderful idea. I'm sorry I'll have to miss it."

Saying "no" does not have to mean the end of the relationship.

• ATTEND EVENT •

Dear Molly,

I appreciate your invitation to join your group for lunch at the Kenmore Foundation and a tour of the new facilities. It must be very satisfying to see all your months of construction finally come to a successful completion.

I'll not be able to attend the lunch, but want to thank you for thinking of me. I wish the foundation much success in all its philanthropic efforts on behalf of our community.

Sincerely,

• ATTEND EVENT—PRIOR COMMITMENT •

Example 1

Dear Todd:

Thank you for the invitation to join the group of friends at your table at the annual Professionals' Prayer Breakfast at the Hyatt on March 28. The speaker lineup sounds impressive. Unfortunately, I'll be in Atlanta that week attending to a key customer account. Otherwise, I'd love the opportunity to meet your colleagues at the table and hear an inspiring message.

Thanks so much for thinking of me. I'll take a rain check for next year.

Regards,

• Attend Event—Prior Commitment •

Example 2

Dear Sherry,

Unexpectedly, my company is sending me to Los Angeles the week of March 9 and requiring me to stay over the weekend for a training session. I'm so disappointed that I'm going to have to miss Gary's wedding. I had already returned my reply card to the bride's family, saying that all four of us would attend. Would you please pass on this development and our regrets?

Give our love and best wishes to Gary and his bride as they start their lives together.

Cordially,

• HEAD PROJECT COMMITTEE—TIME CONFLICT •

Dear Erica,

Your list of potential members for the Economic Development Committee reads like a "Who's Who" of Tyler. I feel flattered that you have invited me to join that illustrious group.

Flattered and disappointed. Disappointed that I can't commit the kind of time this committee work deserves. The projects you outlined as part of the objectives sound truly worthwhile and certainly should attract new corporations to the neighborhood— a prospect that would benefit all of us.

However, this year I've decided to devote all my available time to my continuing work with the symphony. There are still several ongoing projects there that I'd like to complete.

My best wishes as you continue to put together such an all-star lineup.

Regards,

• HOST PARTY—EXPENSE •

Dear Tonya:

The dinner party to honor Mike and Marcy as they move away sounds like a nice idea. I'm sure everyone will want a last opportunity to wish them well on their new venture in Oregon.

Thank you for asking me to join you as host, but I'm afraid I'm going to have to say no because of the expense involved in such an elaborate setting. Johnny and I plan to spend some time with Mike and Marcy individually before they go.

I do know you'll understand, and I hope the event turns out to be a huge success. Mike and Marcy will appreciate your efforts so much.

Cordially,

• LOAN OF PERSONAL ITEM—PERSONAL POLICY •

Dear Linda,

When I returned to town yesterday, I received your message about borrowing some of my crystal bowls and silver serving pieces for the upcoming graduation party.

On occasion, I have let a family member or friend borrow these serving pieces. But the last time a tray was returned chipped, I promised myself I'd not lend them again. Because each piece is a memento from a special trip, I have an emotional attachment to all of them. They really are irreplaceable.

I do hope you understand, and I don't want this to ruin our friendship.

Sincerely,

• Participate in Fund-Raiser—Disagree with Organization •

Dear Mr. Garrett:

I received your personal letter asking for financial contributions to keep the doors of Star Mission open for this coming year. Generally, I look forward to such charitable opportunities, but I must decline on this one.

Frankly, some of the comments from my acquaintances have raised serious doubts about flagrant misuse of funds at the mission. I don't mean illegal use, but simply a misrepresentation about how the money has been used in the past. Also, I have difficulty understanding the mission's philosophy about not imposing a limit on the time that the homeless can stay in the center without seeking training or employment.

For these reasons, I'm reluctant to commit funds. I do wish you success in collecting contributions from those who've had a more positive experience with that organization.

Sincerely,

• SUPPORT POLITICAL CANDIDATE OR ISSUE •

Dear Niada,

Thank you for making me aware of your support for Barbara Lewis in her bid for the newly vacated city council seat.

I've been keenly interested in several of the candidates because of the ongoing problems in the district and have analyzed their positions on several key issues important to the community. Unfortunately, we have differing views on several points. Therefore, I'm going to have to say no to the request that I work in the election campaign and hope that you'll understand my position.

By the way, Ms. Lewis certainly has a cast of admirable backers with the experience you bring to the table on her behalf!

Sincerely,

FRIENDS AND RELATIVES

Some "touchy" situations become even more sensitive when friends or relatives are involved. Those awkward situations include having to remind friends that they promised to write a letter of reference on your behalf, pay for their share of a family gift, or reimburse you for damage done to your belongings. While you want to keep the relationship intact, you still need to remind and motivate people to take some promised or appropriate action. Tone becomes paramount.

State the gist of your message in the opening paragraph: Why are you writing? Don't let this letter ramble into unrelated issues, leaving the relative or friend actually wondering about your overall intention for the letter.

In a negative situation, offer encouragement rather than blame. Don't make the other person feel guilty that things aren't as you hope, expect, or wish. Instead, stick with the situation "as is" and ask for what you need or state your decision about what you can or cannot do to accommodate the other's needs.

When offering encouragement or praise, remember that specific statements sound more genuine than global sentiments. Instead of "I miss you," try "I miss hearing your laugh when we watch TV."

Finally, express your commitment, love, or appreciation despite any problems or negatives in the current situation. A "no" message or a "please do it" message does not have to mean the end of a relationship.

FRIENDLY REMINDERS

• TO CONTACT MUTUAL FRIEND •

Gerri,

Just got a piece of news yesterday—Sandy will be going to New England for the summer to stay with her parents for a long visit. As we agreed, she really needs to hear from you so we can mend fences over the political divisions that developed this winter.

I thought I'd let you know of her plans so you can make contact before she leaves; time only seems to aggravate rather than improve these situations. We've all three had such a positive relationship in the past that I know you're looking forward to getting this present difficulty behind us.

In case you've misplaced it, her address is 232 Lemmons Avenue and her phone number is 333-4242. Thanks for agreeing to get in touch with her.

All best,

• TO FULFILL PROMISE •

Marcia,

My niece, Michelle Travis, and I were having lunch last week and she again mentioned how much she was looking forward to meeting your colleagues at Harris Foundation. Her heart is set on finding a job with a nonprofit organization. And, of course, Harris is the ideal match because of her college major in psychology.

I'm hoping that you're not having difficulty in making suitable arrangements for an informal get-together. If so, may I help in some way? I'd be pleased to schedule a conference room here if you think your colleagues wouldn't mind walking across the street for cocktails and hors d'oeuvres after work some afternoon.

Thanks for your offer to introduce Michelle to your colleagues at the foundation. With the respect this group has for you, you will be doing her a very big favor. We'll both be very appreciative.

Regards,

• TO PAY FOR DAMAGE •

Dear Sherry,

I finally have been able to get the last estimate on re-covering the chair. The bid from Hilton's Upholstery was $545; Graham's Designs quoted $350; and Motley's Designs gave me a figure of $650. (The bids are enclosed.) As you can see, there's quite a difference in price. That difference is probably due to their varying charges for labor and delivery, the fabric price being the same in all cases from the manufacturer.

I was pleased to learn that the manufacturer still had the same fabric in stock, because the chair was purchased so recently. That was the only stroke of luck in this whole unfortunate incident.

I've seen the quality of Graham's work and am, frankly, quite afraid of the final product. I'd feel much more comfortable having Hilton's Upholstery do the work, but I'll do whatever you think is fair. Just make your check payable to me, and I'll pay the company upon completion of the work.

I know you regret as much as I do Jeannie's accident while here, and I appreciate your offer to take care of the damage.

Sincerely,

• To Pay for Share of Gift •

Michael,

Brenda and Ted seemed thrilled with the pottery that our group sent for their Open House. I think they were totally shocked— and so pleased that we thought of them on that occasion, especially since they had dropped their membership a few months ago.

The total tally came to $457, including the shipping charges. That amounts to $50 per couple. You could give me the cash at our next event, but since that won't be until August, I'd really prefer a check (if you don't mind) so we can get this all taken care of. I'd like to report back to the members that all's over and done with it on this end. Just make it payable to either me or Johnny Tuttle.

Thanks for chipping in for the pottery. I really appreciate being able to count on a group as solid as ours.

Regards,

• TO RETURN BORROWED ITEM •

Dear Angela,

Carrie has finally landed a part in the upcoming school theater production, and we're going to be the proud parents mingling with the cast, taking all the irritating photos during the curtain bows and following festivities.

Have you had a chance to pack up all my camera gear yet? I'd appreciate it if you could give me a call and let me know when you can drop it by before "the big week" of April 6.

I hope it served you well on your vacation; we've always liked the way our photos have turned out. But then, of course, it's hard to have operator trouble when all you have to do is push a button.

If this weekend will be convenient for you, we plan to be home.

Regards,

• To Pay Club Dues •

Dear Sarah:

Oops—did you forget? We sent out an earlier notice about annual dues ($45) for our writers' group and had hoped to have all the funds collected by February 1. Our records show that we still have not received your check. Did we miss it somehow?

If so, please let us know the check number and date. If you discover that you have not yet sent your check, please mail it to me directly at 4589 Hanover, Arlington, TX 76015.

As you probably know, we try to keep our dues collection informal and quick because all of us are so busy trying to get that next chapter written. Looking forward to seeing you at the next meeting. We have some great programs lined up for this coming year.

Sincerely,

PERSONAL LOANS

• REQUESTING LOAN FROM FRIEND OR RELATIVE •

Dear Uncle Max,

I'm writing under difficult circumstances. I've had a recent car accident and the police totaled my car. Thank goodness, no one was hurt. But my primary concern now is finding transportation to and from work. I've located a used car for $2000 from a colleague at work, but I haven't yet worked long enough to be able to save that kind of money.

Would you consider lending me the $2000 to buy the car? I can repay the loan at $150 a month until it is paid in full. I'd be more than willing to pay interest on the loan also.

As you may be aware, there's no metro bus or subway service in this part of the country, and I'm in danger of losing my job if I can't find dependable transportation. I've tried to get a loan at my local bank, but all my credit reports still show the evidences of my college escapades 4 years ago. Although I learned my lesson about handling easy credit long ago, the bank has nothing but my word to prove it. If you will consider the loan, please let me know and I'll telephone my colleague before she sells the car to someone else. If not, I'll understand.

Sincerely,

P.S. I'm writing rather than phoning to give you ample time to consider my request before giving me an answer.

• PROMISING REPAYMENT TO FRIEND OR RELATIVE •

Dear Nancy,

Whatever you do, don't assume that I've forgotten about the $300 I borrowed from you for car repairs.

I am sorry that I haven't yet repaid you, but I *will* do so. By the end of the month, you should have received at least half the money. And within a few weeks after that, you'll have the other half too.

Meanwhile, rest assured that I am watching every penny until my debt is settled. Thanks for your patience with me.

Sincerely,

• GRANTING LOAN TO FRIEND OR RELATIVE •

Dear Lanny,

As we discussed on the phone last night, I'm enclosing a check for $2000 for your car purchase. Also, I've computed the interest rate we discussed and have drafted a note to confirm your repayment arrangements on the last day of each month. Please keep a copy for yourself and sign and return a copy.

Through the years, I've found that having a written confirmation of what everyone has agreed to makes things clear for all concerned. All my best with the car. Keep in touch.

Your Uncle Max

• REQUESTING REPAYMENT •

Jason,

Have you "settled into" your new job by now, and do you still feel as enthusiastic about it as you did at the beginning? Of course, any job has its drudgery tasks, but all in all, from what you told us, it sounds like a good match for you.

We're writing to ask when we can expect repayment of the $1500 loan for your car. We were glad to help you with the purchase of your Toyota so that you'd have transportation back and forth to your new job. You agreed to pay all, or at least half, of the loan by June. If you have decided that you cannot repay the total $1500 at once, we understand. But we do need to receive at least half that amount within the next 2 or 3 weeks.

We hope the car you selected has not disappointed you. We, too, thought it was a good buy. Please let us know how things are going.

Sincerely,

• DECLINING REQUEST FOR LOAN FROM FRIEND OR RELATIVE •

Dear Sandra,

I appreciate your sharing your current financial difficulties with me. I understand how disappointed you must feel about the unexpected expenses in your first few months in operation.

Now that I've had time to think over the situation, I've decided that I must say no on the loan. Personal loans have always been "off limits" with me, because so many good relationships have been broken over this issue.

Starting your own business is always risky, I guess. I've never had the courage to venture out on my own as you have. I hope you will accept my answer as nothing personal—just a reflection of my own philosophy about friendship and finances.

Sincerely,

GOVERNMENT PROGRAMS

From time to time, you will have to contact government agencies about Medicare, social security, or veterans' issues for yourself or on behalf of your loved ones. And dealing with government agencies can be exasperating because of the sheer volume of letters these agencies receive. That is, their volume of correspondence means that you will likely receive a form response—and often an inaccurate or inappropriate one—unless you take special care to provide all necessary information and ask questions specifically about your situation.

To lessen the likelihood of incomplete information or repeat requests, use a reference line to identify yourself before you begin the body of your letter: social security number, case number, account number, member number, or any other identifying information for quick reference to a previous file and related data. Such a reference will help supply the government employee with all the available information in interpreting regulations pertinent to your situation.

Try to summarize your message or request in a sentence or two at the beginning of your letter:

"I'm writing to ask for the status on…"

"I need information about…"

"Would you please provide information about X and any necessary forms and guidelines to take this action?"

Provide supporting detail of your position or request. Answer the 6 W's questions: who, what, when, where, why, how, how much. Let your reader know that you will not settle for a general response in a form letter. Make it clear that you expect a direct answer/interpretation/decision for your specific situation rather than a general citing of a written policy or law. For example:

> *"Would you please answer these two specific questions as they apply to my situation? First…"*
>
> *"Am I or am I not eligible for these benefits?"*
>
> *"The earlier form letter I received did not provide a full explanation of how this policy applies to my situation. Specifically, I need to know…"*

Finally, include written documentation of past action, claims, notifications, or requests.

Persistence pays.

MEDICARE

• REQUESTING INFORMATION ABOUT AVAILABLE HEALTH AND HUMAN SERVICES •

U.S. Department of Health and Human Services

Would you please send information about government services or resources available to me because of (*physical condition, death of family member, immigration, and so forth*)?

Also, I'd like to have the name, address, and phone number of any regional offices nearby that I may decide to visit or contact about this issue.

Sincerely,

• REQUESTING STATEMENT OF EARNINGS •

U.S. Department of Health and Human Services

Dear Sir or Madam:

I will be 65 on my next birthday, and need to have information about my eligibility for social security and Medicare benefits, along with the procedure and forms to apply for these benefits.

To verify my eligibility and compute my likely earnings, I'd like to receive a copy of earnings that have been attributed to me during my employment years.

The pertinent identification details follow:

Full current legal name: Maya Allison Smothers
Maiden name: Maya Allison Burnett
Former married name: Maya Allison Burnett Carter
Social security number: 123-45-6789

Thank you for your prompt response in sending the appropriate forms and procedures to begin these benefits.

Sincerely,

• REQUESTING LIST OF PHYSICIANS •

Dear Medicare Representative:

As a recently retired widower, I am now enrolled in Medicare. Would you please send me a list of physicians and facilities in my local area that accept Medicare assignment for the health services they provide?

Sincerely,

• REPORTING INCORRECT BILLING •

RE: Invoice Number 234890

Dear Dr. Jahns:

Your office sent me an incorrect statement for my recent treatment of gastrointestinal tests done the week of May 5. Would you please send a corrected statement for the service?

Your office submitted the claim directly to Medicare for me, and Medicare has paid its limits on these services. Your bill still shows an outstanding balance of $92 due from the patient. It was my understanding that you accepted the Medicare limits as total payment for these services, rather than charging your typical fee for these tests. I appreciate the seniors' discount for this service, and evidently this recent billing to me for the "difference" between the insurance payment and the full fee is an inadvertent error on the part of your staff.

Thank you for your competent medical services. I'll appreciate a correct invoice and will forward my check immediately.

Sincerely,

• DISPUTING DENIAL OF BENEFITS •

RE: Case Number 78333

Dear Mr. DeVargas:

I'm asking for a reversal of your earlier decision to deny benefits to my mother, Alma Simpson, for hospitalization for her gastrointestinal testing procedures.

We understand that this normally is an outpatient procedure. However, because of my mother's medical history of internal bleeding and complications with heart ailments, she clearly needs to be hospitalized for this testing. Enclosed is a copy of her medical history, including ailments and treatment dates, along with a letter from her attending physician about the advisability of hospitalization for this current testing.

Please reassess this situation and respond to me about allowing coverage for the hospitalization that her current condition warrants during this testing procedure. We would appreciate your immediate response, because my mother's condition grows worse by the day.

Sincerely,

SOCIAL SECURITY

• APPLYING FOR SOCIAL SECURITY CARD •

Social Security Administration

Dear Sir or Madam:

I want to apply for a social security card for my minor child. Please send the necessary information and forms to me at the above address.

Sincerely,

• APPLYING FOR BENEFITS •

Social Security Administration

RE: Social Security Number 333-33-3333

Dear Sir or Madam:

My husband Ralph T. Michaels is terminally ill, and I am writing to determine what benefits my two minor children and I will be eligible for under social security at his death. My husband's social security number is listed above.

Sincerely,

• CHANGING NAME AFTER MARRIAGE •

Social Security Administration

RE: Social Security Number 456-98-9889
    Mary Beth Crabapple (maiden) Robinson

I recently married and need to have my social security records changed to my married name: Mary Beth Robinson. Enclosed is a copy of my marriage certificate. Please send me the appropriate forms to complete this change and let me know of any other supporting documentation required.

Sincerely,

• CHANGING NAME AFTER DIVORCE •

Social Security Administration

RE: Social Security Number 444-44-4444
    Leanne Gaither Medicalf

I have recently divorced and need to have my name changed on your social security records. Would you please send me a replacement card also? (A copy of the old card and the divorce decree is enclosed.) Please issue the new card in the name of Leanne Medicalf at the above address.

Sincerely,

• REQUESTING DIRECT DEPOSIT OF CHECKS •

Social Security Administration

RE: Social Security Number 777-77-7777

Dear Social Security Administration Representative:

My social security checks are now coming to my home at 457 Lassiter Road, Colleyville, TX 76034, and I would like to change this arrangement and have them deposited directly into my bank account:

Account Number 490093331
BankNow
38894 Arbor Road
Arlington, TX 76031

Please either make this change immediately or send me the appropriate forms to do so.

Sincerely,

• CANCELING DIRECT DEPOSIT OF CHECKS •

Social Security Administration

RE: Social Security Number 777-77-7777

Dear Representative:

My social security checks are currently deposited directly into my bank account: Account Number 490093331, BankNow, 38894 Arbor Road, Arlington, TX 76031.

I'd like to change that arrangement and have the checks come directly to my new home at 457 Lassiter Road, Colleyville, TX 76034, effective with the *June check.*

Please either make this change immediately or send me the appropriate forms to do so.

Sincerely,

• REPORTING CHANGE OF ADDRESS •

Social Security Administration

RE: Social Security Number 777-77-7777

Dear Social Security Administration Representative:

I need to change the mailing address for my social security checks, effective immediately.

Current Address: 457 Lassiter Road
                 Colleyville, TX 76034

New Address: 9355 Trail Lakes
                 Fort Worth, TX 76180

Please either make this change immediately or send me the appropriate forms to do so.

Sincerely,

• NOTIFYING ADMINISTRATION OF DEATH OF SPOUSE •

Social Security Administration

RE: Social Security Numbers
   Cassandra Adams: 555-55-5555
   Don Adams: 666-66-6666

Dear Sir or Madam:

My wife, Cassandra Adams, died on October 5. Her monthly social security benefit was $689 at the time of her death. I am writing to determine my eligibility for survivor's benefits. Her death certificate is enclosed.

Please send me the necessary forms and information for applying for these benefits. My address remains the same as on the letterhead above.

Sincerely,

• REPORTING LOST OR STOLEN SOCIAL SECURITY CARD •

Social Security Administration

RE: Social Security Number 888-88-8888

My social security card has been lost. Would you please send me the appropriate forms and guidelines to receive a replacement card? My current address is 3888 Billings Street, Tallahassee, FL 32399.

Sincerely,

• REQUESTING STATEMENT OF EARNINGS OR BENEFITS •

Social Security Administration

Please send the form *Request for Earnings and Benefit Estimate Statement* to me at the above address.

Sincerely,

• DISPUTING AMOUNT OF ENTITLEMENT •

Social Security Administration

RE: Social Security Number 222-22-2222

Dear Representative:

There seems to be some mistake in your computation of my social security benefits. I received my first check (a copy enclosed) for $758, almost $120 less than the amount that your earlier letter (copy enclosed) reported that I would receive.

Please review your records, clarify the correct amount, and send me a copy of your computations and figures used in the formula.

Sincerely,

• DISPUTING DENIAL OF BENEFITS •

Social Security Administration

RE: Social Security Number 123-45-6789

Dear Sir or Madam:

I recently received notice that my social security benefits have been terminated because my wages from part-time employment exceed the specified limits.

Before I accepted the new job, I inquired with your office and was assured that my $6-per-hour job (total monthly income $180) was well under the limits. Obviously, someone gave me incorrect information or your recent termination action was inappropriate.

Please review the situation, and forward the outstanding checks immediately. Copies of your termination notice and my last check stubs are enclosed.

Sincerely,

VETERANS' AFFAIRS

• REQUESTING MILITARY RECORDS •

Personnel Records Center

RE: Service Number/Social Security Number 334-89-9997

Dear Military Official:

I have been unable to locate the original copy of my discharge papers from the Navy. Would you please send a duplicate copy to the above address?

My full name is Susan Gregory Wyatt. I served in the National Guard from May 1989 to March 1994.

Thank you for an immediate response. This verification is necessary for a scholarship application for the upcoming fall semester.

Sincerely,

• REQUESTING CIVIL SERVICE PREFERENCE CERTIFICATE •

RE: Service Number 455-69-9984

Ladies or Gentlemen:

I understand that I may be entitled to special employment considerations because I am a veteran of the Desert Storm era and recently completed my active duty assignment (service dates: April 1989 to April 1995).

Would you please provide a Civil Service Preference Certificate to be included with my job application at the oil company with which I'm seeking employment?

If there are any forms I must complete, please send them, along with any published information or testing requirements that may help me should I decide to seek civil service employment opportunities.

Sincerely,

• REQUESTING VA-GUARANTEED LOAN •

RE: Service Number 09983
      Social Security Number 389-55-9999

Dear Representative:

I plan to purchase a new home in the next few months and would like verification of my eligibility for a VA-guaranteed loan and general information about the loan (guidelines, restrictions, current mortgage rates, and so forth).

I served in the Army from March 1962 to April 1964. I received an honorable discharge and left the Army with the rank of captain.

Please forward information and forms to the above address. I'll appreciate a quick response, because a house-purchase decision is pending.

Sincerely,

• REQUESTING EXCHANGE AND COMMISSARY PRIVILEGES •

RE: Spouse's Service Number 333-55-5555

Dear Administrator:

I understand that as a widow of a veteran who suffered a disability in connection to his service in the U.S. Army during the Bosnia operations I may be entitled to privileges through the local exchange and commissary.

Would you please send me the appropriate form to apply for these privileges and receive an identification card? Thank you.

Sincerely,

• REQUESTING REIMBURSEMENT FOR BURIAL MONUMENT •

Dear Administrator:

My husband, James J. Timmons, died on April 29 and was buried at Heartland Memorial Gardens here in Omaha, Nebraska. We purchased a gravesite marker for $855. I understand that the family is entitled to reimbursement for an "average" cost for a government marker.

Would you please either process this reimbursement or send the necessary forms to complete so that we may receive this reimbursement?

The pertinent details regarding my husband's service follow:

Branch: Marines
Dates of Service: October 1, 1984, to December 1, 1988
Discharge: Honorable

I've enclosed a copy of his death certificate and a copy of the receipt for our purchase of the gravestone from C. C. Rosenburg Funeral Home.

Sincerely,

• CLAIMING INSURANCE BENEFITS •

RE: Service Number/Social Security Number 666-45-4444
     Life Insurance Policy 44494949494

My husband, Allan C. Pence, passed away on March 15 of this year. Would you please let me know what benefits or disbursements I'm entitled to as surviving spouse and beneficiary to his life insurance policy:

Date of Birth: 2/12/46

Branch of Service: Army

Service Dates: 2/27/64 to 2/26/94

Rank: Lieutenant Colonel

Discharge: Honorable

Enclosed is a certified copy of his death certificate. Thank you for your prompt response about disbursement of the life insurance benefits.

Sincerely,

• DISPUTING DENIAL OF BENEFITS •

RE: Service Number 394-55-8888

Dear Veterans' Office Representative:

I received a letter from your office, saying that my recent claim for additional compensation had been denied. It appears that the letter is a form letter and does not disclose the reason that I was denied the additional bonus pay for having completed the 14-month language training program with a passing grade.

Therefore, I am requesting a review of this claim and a full, specific explanation about the reasons for the denial. If I do not receive a reversal of this decision, I plan to file an appeal within the required time frame to follow up on my rightful claim to this bonus.

All appropriate documentation is enclosed (service letter explaining the language bonus, grades, my original letter to you, your form letter to me).

I expect to hear from you immediately about this review and to receive the full compensation due me under this recruitment arrangement.

Sincerely,

HOME CONCERNS

Unfortunately, you can't leave all your problems at the office. As a homeowner or renter, you will undoubtedly be faced with neighborhood or environmental concerns. You'll be negotiating to buy, sell, lease, or evict. You'll need repairs completed. You'll have to move and handle associated details, from address changes to utility refunds. And as a landlord of rental property, you'll have to handle two sets of books and correspondence on all the above.

Keep in mind these general guidelines: Summarize your message or request in the opening sentence or two. Then provide specific details on effective dates, fees and payments, names, and addresses.

Ask specifically for what you want and add a deadline for response, if appropriate. If you become embroiled in a conflict, show your willingness to compromise, if appropriate, to meet all parties' needs:

> *"I can arrange to alter my school schedule to be there to let the repairperson into the house if you can give me a specific time."*
>
> *"I would be willing to forfeit $100 of my deposit if you could release me from the contract and find a suitable tenant by that date."*
>
> *"I understand your needing to keep the apartments leased and am trying to work out some compromise that will meet my needs as well."*

Remember to enclose copies of related documents to make the reader's verification or action quick and easy.

Neighborhood and environmental issues will be of special concern and deserve special handling. Summarize the issue or the situation. State why it is dangerous to you or the community. Finally, be clear about what action (or inaction) you want the reader to take. Convey the attitude that you assume the reader will make attempts to correct the problem or improve the situation once he or she becomes aware of the hazard.

Generally, you should refrain from making specific threats unless you are prepared to carry them out. In a negative and recurring situation, simply state what other options you will be forced to consider:

"If I don't hear from you, I will be forced to contact the proper authorities."

"Frankly, if I have to contact a lawyer, it may cost me more than the repairs, but I'm determined to do that if that's what it takes to get this matter resolved."

"I'm hoping you can meet your commitment so that we can avoid any legal action in this situation."

"I'm hopeful that you can install the new heater before I have to escalate the problem further."

"I will wait to hear of your decision before I notify the owner about the situation."

"I hope no further action will be necessary."

"Any further correspondence should be directed to my lawyer at..."

Home is where the heart is, so you'll want to make sure you keep the hearth burning brightly by taking care of all the persistent and pesky concerns that plague renters and homeowners.

NEIGHBORHOOD AND ENVIRONMENTAL CONCERNS

• REQUESTING ROAD REPAIR •

Dear Mr. Gottlieb:

I want to warn you of a problem about which you may be unaware. The potholes in the service road near my office are as dangerous as they are maddening. I cannot tell you how many times I have seen a near-accident on this road as cars and trucks swerve to avoid the holes. In the interest of safety, I beg you to please do what you can to address this potentially disastrous problem.

The stretch of service road to which I refer is on the westbound side of Highway 183 between Shallot Avenue and Geller Lane. I work in the Enterprise Building at 503 Geller Lane, on the northwest corner of Geller and 183.

A number of my coworkers and I have discussed this predicament of the potholes repeatedly. I have also overheard disgruntled grumbles about it in the lobby, on the elevator, and in the café that is located inside the Enterprise Building. We are all anxious to see this problem remedied.

To signify to you the magnitude of our discontent, I have enclosed a petition signed by the staff of the entire Enterprise Building. Mr. Gottlieb, we would all be deeply grateful if you could give this issue the much-needed attention it deserves.

Respectfully yours,

• PROTESTING POLLUTION •

Dear Mrs. Wang:

I have just had my tap water tested for various contamination levels and am aghast at the increase in the amount of heavy metals in our local water source. Such contaminants can lead to any one of a number of long-term illnesses, to decreased mental capacity over a long period of time, and even to birth defects. We must do something about the quality of our drinking water.

I implore you, for the sake of our families, our friends, the environment, and the generations yet to be, to tackle this problem now! We need your help, Mrs. Wang. We need action. Cite those responsible for the environmental violations. Provide guidelines for cleanup. Insist that people meet them lest they incur additional fines. Stand up to their economic power.

I have done some research on the origin of the pollution of our water source. Not surprisingly, the decline in our water quality coincides with the inception of the new Ashlake facility in our area in 1989. Here is a company that has received countless citations, including several multimillion-dollar fines for environmental degradation. The EPA and the state of Virginia have both repeatedly demanded that the company clean up its act. Yet it is cheaper for Ashlake to pay the fines as just another business expense. If this reckless treatment of the environment is to be curbed, the fines must be large enough to hurt Ashlake's profit margin.

I have circulated an informative memo on this exigency to residents in the area. I will include it here so that you too may increase your awareness of our dire circumstances. Please take this seriously. If we don't do something immediately, the consequences could be devastating for all of us.

Very respectfully yours,

• PROTESTING CITY PLANNING •

Dear Mr. Kutzler:

I find Dallas–Fort Worth's plans to expand the airport for 5 square miles southward absolutely disturbing. I live in northeast Tarrant County, where already an occasionally low-flying plane rattles my windows as it thunders toward the nearby runway. Should the airport planners have their way at the zoning hearing and be allowed to construct more landing strips 5 miles even closer to my house, I'm afraid that what remains of our suburban tranquility here will disappear.

Mr. Kutzler, as the chairperson of the Zoning Commission, you should be informed of all pertinent opinions with regard to this issue. Speaking for myself and an entire community's worth of potentially irate families, I strongly encourage you to decline DFW's request for southward expansion.

I live in the 2400 block of Trinity Boulevard in Arlington. It is a relatively peaceful neighborhood, which was a key factor in my husband's and my decision to buy our house back in 1990. At that time, we were told that zoning ordinances prevented the airport from expanding in our direction.

I have enclosed a copy of the zoning ordinance that was designed to preclude any such construction; it is still current. Please don't amend it in order to accommodate DFW's airport. It was this piece of legislation that convinced us to move into the neighborhood 6 years ago. I don't want it to be the reason we take a loss on our house and leave our neighbors this year.

Sincerely,

• REQUESTING ZONING VARIANCE •

Dear Board Members:

We recently purchased property in the Trail Lakes Estate of the city. In talking with the architect preparing our house plans, I was told that the city has specified no side-entrance garages. I'd like to request a variance on this ruling to permit such a structure.

The original decision was made to ensure that homes left adequate space for city sidewalks that might possibly surround the complete large-acre lots. The esthetics of the situation demanded that pedestrians on the sidewalks not see into others' garages. However, the situation has changed. All homes in the subdivision are now complete, and no such "surrounding" sidewalks have been constructed.

My neighbors, the only people that this issue affects, have no objection to the side-entrance garage, and their signed statements to that effect are attached.

If you will approve this variance, please send me the written documentation immediately in the enclosed self-addressed, stamped envelope. If I need to complete any forms, please include those as well. Thank you for your prompt attention to this matter; my wife and I are eager to move ahead with our housing plans.

Sincerely,

BUYING AND SELLING

• Requesting Amortization Schedule of Payments •

RE: Loan Number 388355

Dear Miss Burdette:

My husband and I have a mortgage with your company for our home at 4689 Windy Way Circle. Would you please send me a new amortization schedule of payments from the start of the loan? We want to verify the calculations since we made our lump-sum payment of $35,000 last month against the principal.

Sincerely,

• REQUESTING PAYOFF OF BALANCE OF MORTGAGE •

RE: Home Mortgage Loan 8889300

Dear Loan Officer:

We intend to pay off the mortgage on our home at 4998 Bristol Avenue on March 9. Please provide us with the payoff balance on this loan as of that date. Our contract shows no penalty for an early payoff. Would you please verify that issue also in your response to us?

Finally, would you let us know if any amount of escrow money for taxes and insurance will be refunded at the time of payoff?

Thank you for a prompt response; we have a pending sale.

Sincerely,

• ENLISTING REAL ESTATE AGENT •

Dear Mr. Miller:

We are considering putting our home at 8945 Brentway on the market in February and are investigating various real estate agencies with experience in this locale. Previously, we had our home up for sale about 2 years ago for $198,000, and the listing agent at that time made very little effort, in our opinion, to sell the home, although she suggested that listing price. We had no offers during the entire 6-month period, and only one potential buyer came to see the house.

If you would be interested in selling the home, would you please run comparable prices for recent home sales in our neighborhood and send us a copy of your standard 3- to 6-month listing agreement? After we review this information, if we are still interested in moving ahead with the listing, we'll phone to ask that you meet us here to inspect the property.

Sincerely,

• THANKING REAL ESTATE AGENT •

Dear Sheri,

Now that the boxes are unpacked and the dust has settled in our new home, we want to thank you for handling both the sale of our Overlake property and the purchase of our new home in Montclair Parc.

In a nutshell, you were thoroughly up to date in your knowledge of the market, adept at interviewing us to identify the criteria most important in selling our home as well as in building a new one, creative in identifying potential buyers, aggressive in your follow-up calls to potential buyers who looked at the home, and finally attentive to all the details throughout the 9-month process on both homes. And, of course, we appreciate the little extras—like selling our used refrigerator to another client couple and setting up the appointment to introduce us to potential customers for our consulting business. Finally, after-the-sale service is important to us; you continue to come through in that regard with the last-minute items still needing attention from our builder.

Please feel free to use our name as a reference for any potential home buyers or sellers. We can have nothing but good things to say about the extra effort you made in making sure we were satisfied. Thank you for your efforts on our behalf. Now we know why you're consistently among the top agents in the region!

Sincerely,

• CANCELING REAL ESTATE LISTING WITH AGENT •

Dear Ms. Wong:

Please consider this letter as notification that when our listing expires on April 1, we do not plan to renew the agreement with your agency. As you know, we have been very disappointed in the efforts you've made to call attention to the property. We do not consider a sign in the yard as appropriate advertising for our out-of-the-way location.

We also think the asking price that you suggested is off target and suspect that you intended to recommend our lowering the price with your renewal for another 6 months. However, we cannot afford the luxury of a long wait for that ideal buyer. As we first explained, we must sell our home immediately—at a reasonable price.

Sincerely,

• WITHDRAWING OFFER TO PURCHASE •

Dear Mr. Coker:

With this letter, we are withdrawing our offer of $258,000 to purchase the property at 811 Bellview Court. Since there has been no response in the past 3 days either to accept or to reject our offer, we ask that you simply void the contract immediately.

Sincerely,

HOME REPAIR AND IMPROVEMENT

• REQUESTING INFORMATION ABOUT PERMIT FOR IMPROVEMENTS •

Dear City Inspector:

We are planning to construct an 8-foot wooden fence around our investment property at 3499 Glennlake. The area is zoned as residential, although there are no other houses under construction. Do we have the city's permission to proceed with that construction?

We are unaware of any code restrictions. If a special permit is necessary, would you please forward to us the appropriate forms?

Sincerely,

• REQUESTING PRICE QUOTE •

Dear Mr. Vonnegut:

Your representative, Fred Simmons, dropped by our home last Friday to give us an estimate on recarpeting our floors. At that time, he measured our home, but did not give us a complete estimate for total installation, with padding and labor charges added.

Would you please provide in writing your quote for recarpeting our home in all the same rooms that are now carpeted? Please include in the quote your total fee for our carpet selection at $22 per square foot, including the highest-grade quality for your padding and all labor charges.

Also, would you please mention in your quote any guarantees you offer and provide a list of three or four customers we may call for references?

Thank you for your time in providing this bid. We hope to make a decision by midmonth.

Sincerely,

MOVING

• COMPLAINING ABOUT MOVERS •

RE: Invoice 8900933

Dear Mr. Arnold:

We are writing to make you aware of the difficulties we had when your staff handled our move from 1010 West Ryan Road to 2598 Towering Oaks. The movers arrived late and wasted time during the day on several "breaks," several items were damaged, and the move took two days rather than the promised one day.

We expect immediate payment for the damaged items and a refund of $280 for the excessive hours charged for labor.

As you will see from the enclosed estimate from your sales representative, Cindy Nowells, your movers (four of them) were to arrive at 8:00 a.m. the day of the move and work until the local move was complete. Ms. Nowells estimated the move would take 9 hours at a fee of $160 per hour. The first two movers arrived at 8:15; the last two movers arrived at 9:00. During the day, they took a 2-hour lunch break and then several breaks randomly, during which time the rest of the crew slowed their pace "to wait for help." Consequently, they did not finish the move at the estimated time and had to return the second day for three hours to unload the truck completely. This delay was another unplanned inconvenience.

Additionally, four paintings were damaged when the movers packed them in the flat cardboard boxes. They decided that crating the pictures was unnecessary because of the short-distance move. When the movers unboxed them upon arrival, the glass was cracked on each of the four and the frames were scratched.

(Continued)

I've enclosed your completed claims form, along with purchase receipts for the pictures, and a copy of your original estimate, showing the estimated total weight of our household goods.

Please give this matter your immediate attention. We expect full and prompt settlement of this claim.

Sincerely,

• CANCELING ACCOUNT WITH UTILITY—REFUND DEPOSIT •

RE: Utilities at 810 Busier Lane

Please cancel our electricity service at 810 Busier Lane, effective May 10. You can refund our deposit to the above *new* address.

Sincerely,

• CANCELING ACCOUNT WITH UTILITY—TRANSFER DEPOSIT •

RE: 810 Busier Lane

We are moving from 810 Busier Lane to 4900 Hogan Avenue on May 1. Please cancel our electricity at Busier Lane on May 1, and begin our service at Hogan Avenue on the same day.

Please transfer our deposit from the old address to the new address. If a deposit is no longer required because of our on-time payment record during the past 4 years, would you please refund that deposit to me at my new address?

Sincerely,

• CHANGING ADDRESS WITH FAMILY OR FRIENDS •

We've moved!

And we wouldn't want to miss any of those invitations, announcements, or periodic updates of what's going on in your life, so please make a note of our new address. While you're at it, write and let us hear from you!

5206 Orville Avenue
Laurenceville, GA 30244
(404) 985-1891

RENTER'S CONCERNS

• COMPLAINING ABOUT PROPERTY EMPLOYEE •

Dear Mr. Mattox:

I want to let you know of my concern about the behavior of one of your maintenance people, Ralph Clark. On two occasions last week, I passed Mr. Clark as he was repairing the fence near the swimming pool. On both occasions, he made suggestive remarks to me, which I tried to ignore without acknowledgment.

Then last Friday, May 3, Mr. Clark unexpectedly knocked on my door, saying he was sent to check the thermostat. When I told him that I had not called for repairs, he mumbled something about having the wrong apartment but then stayed to try to engage me in conversation. Again, I told him I was busy and terminated the conversation.

Would you please talk with Mr. Clark about the suggestive remarks at the pool, and then verify that he indeed did have a call to check a thermostat last Friday. This behavior causes me concern about my safety here. I'd appreciate your phoning me in the evening (457-8885) to let me know the outcome of your conversation.

Sincerely,

• PROTESTING RENT INCREASE •

Dear Manager:

I received your notice about the rent increase of $80 a month, effective July 1, and I strongly protest this increase on behalf of my fellow tenants.

We understand that your costs for taxes and maintenance have increased, but living costs have escalated for all of us as well. Many of us as tenants were promised new installation of carpet when we signed our leases. My carpet, as yet, has not been replaced, nor has that of those renters to whom I spoke about the issue.

Please give me the specific date of carpet installation. If that installation has not been scheduled, we strongly urge you to reconsider the effective date of the rent increase. Otherwise, many of us will be forced to seek other living arrangements when our leases expire.

Sincerely,

• REQUESTING APARTMENT SUBLET •

Dear Mr. Condor:

My company has unexpectedly notified me that I will be transferred to New York on April 30. As you know, my apartment lease runs until June 1 of next year, and I must find a way to handle that commitment.

Although your contract doesn't provide for a sublease arrangement, I'm requesting that you make an exception in this case, since my lease runs for another 14 months. I plan to announce the apartment availability on my company's bulletin board and run an ad in the newsletter. I feel certain that I can find a suitable tenant immediately.

Because I will be ultimately responsible for on-time payments, I guarantee that I will take utmost care in finding a responsible, creditworthy tenant.

If you will not allow such an arrangement, I have an alternative suggestion: I'd like to pay you an extra month's rent at the end of April in exchange for an early release from my contract. That extra month's rent will allow you time to find a suitable tenant yourself.

I've been very pleased living in your apartment complex this past year and will recommend it highly to my colleagues moving into the area. Would you please let me have your decision about the subleasing or the early-cancellation arrangement as soon as possible?

Thank you for considering these options.

Sincerely,

• REMINDER OF REQUEST TO REPAIR APARTMENT (WITHHOLDING RENT) •

Dear Ms. Ford:

My cooking range in Apartment 322 is still not working properly. I have phoned you twice (May 2 and May 8) and written once (May 16) to ask that you send a maintenance person to check it (the burners on the left don't heat at all). I mentioned that I would be home in the evenings after 7 and all day Saturday. To my knowledge, no one has been by to make the repair.

If the range is not working by June 1, I will be forced to escrow a portion of my rent until the burners have been repaired or replaced. Should such an arrangement become necessary, I will deposit the escrowed rent with my lawyer and you can contact him when you've completed the repairs.

I hope that you will complete the promised repairs and that this escrow action becomes unnecessary. My cooking range is not an "extra," but rather an essential appliance; I eat most of my meals at home. Please complete the repairs immediately.

Sincerely,

• VACATING PROPERTY •

Dear Manager:

I plan to vacate Apartment 450 in the Villa Capri Complex at 5400 Lawndale on October 15. Please let me know the prorated rent to that date so that I can prepare my final payment accordingly.

After final inspection, you can mail my deposit to me at 3445 Runner's Circle, Apartment 230, Pacifica, CA 94044. I will be leaving the apartment clean and all appliances in good working condition.

Sincerely,

• Terminating Lease •

Dear Manager:

I am terminating my lease on Apartment 14 at Haven Living on Fuller Parkway. This letter provides a full 60-day notice, as required by the lease contract.

After I secure another apartment closer to my new job, I'll let you know where you can mail the deposit refund. There has been no damage to the apartment, and I'm anticipating a full refund.

Thank you for efficient responses to all requests for repairs during my tenure in the apartment.

Sincerely,

• REQUESTING RETURN OF DEPOSIT •

Dear Manager:

When I vacated Apartment 350 in Mellon Manor on Arbor Street, I was denied a refund of my initial $450 deposit because the apartment was not vacuumed and the bathrooms not cleaned. At the time of checkout, Mr. Vegas, the local manager, provided an inventory showing that all appliances were intact and working properly and noted only the unclean apartment as the reason for refusing the refund.

I cleaned the apartment the next day, requested a reinspection, and was told by Mr. Vegas that he would mail the deposit check. The check has never arrived, although I've made three follow-up calls to his office.

Please check into this matter immediately and mail the deposit refund to me at the address above. Otherwise, I'll be forced to report this issue to the Better Business Bureau and escalate the matter for appropriate legal action.

Sincerely,

LANDLORD'S CONCERNS

• NOTIFYING TENANTS OF RENT INCREASE •

Dear Tenants:

Much to our chagrin, the taxes on our apartment complex have been reassessed and increased by 15 percent this past year. To offset these additional costs, we find it necessary to increase rent as detailed in the attached flyer, which gives current and new rates for each building location, floor, and size.

This new amount will go into effect with your rental payments due on July 1. We regret the increase, but want to be able to continue to provide you with the same amenities you've become accustomed to at Buena Vista.

Thank you for your cooperation, and we look forward to continuing to make your apartment living comfortable and safe.

Sincerely,

• NOTIFYING TENANTS OF SALE OF PROPERTY •

Dear Tenants:

I have just completed sale of the condominium in which you are residing to T. R. Stone and Associates. Effective with your October payment, you should mail your rent checks directly to the new owner at the following address:

T. R. Stone and Associates
P.O. Box 499
Nashville, TN 37234

Thank you for your cooperation and prompt payments while I owned the building.

Sincerely,

• REQUESTING TENANT TO REMOVE PET •

Dear Mr. Tanner:

Last Friday, when my son-in-law was in your apartment to repair the dryer outlet, he noticed evidence of a dog in your premises. This letter is to remind you that your lease prohibits pets in the apartment.

Please remove the dog immediately and permanently from the apartment. We will be checking the premises on or before March 10 to ensure that you have complied with the terms of your lease agreement. We will expect your full cooperation.

Sincerely,

• REQUESTING TENANT TO PAY FOR DAMAGES •

Dear Mr. and Mrs. Gardner:

When we drove by your house last week, we noticed that the front lawn and row of hedges around the driveway have been damaged. Thank you for your responsiveness and honesty in our phone conversation about the matter on August 10. We know you regret that your summer houseguests have wreaked such havoc with your yard in your absence.

However, your house lease with us clearly states that you are responsible for any damage to the house as a result of the behavior of your guests. We regret that your houseguests have not been as responsible as you have been during your time with us, and regret to have to tell you again that you are ultimately responsible for the damage.

We can arrange to have the lawn and hedge replaced through our landscaper and have him bill you directly, or you can select the landscaper of your choice—so long as the lawn and hedge are of comparable look and value as the original landscaping. We need to approve any changes to the original design.

Please let us know which way you plan to handle the situation.

Sincerely,

• WARNING NOISY TENANT OF COMPLAINTS •

Dear Ms. Howard:

Several of your neighbors continue to complain about the noise coming from inside your apartment and from your back patio during weekend parties. We, of course, do not care to dictate what goes on in your apartment. But when your behavior and that of your guests infringes on the rights of other tenants to a quiet environment, then we must insist on a change.

Please consider this warning carefully. If we continue to receive other complaints and our investigations prove them to be valid, we will have no choice but to terminate your lease immediately without further warning.

We hope you'll be able to change the disruptive situation.

Sincerely,

• WARNING TENANT ABOUT DELINQUENT RENT •

Dear Mr. and Mrs. George:

For the past several months, your rent payments have been late, arriving even 5 to 10 days past the "grace period" provided in your lease agreement.

This letter will serve as a reminder that your rent in full is due on the first day of each month. If you are having a temporary difficulty, please make us aware of the problem. Otherwise, we'll expect to have your rent on time, as agreed when you assumed occupancy of the duplex.

We appreciate your full cooperation so that no other action will be necessary.

Sincerely,

INVITATIONS

Often, the most pressing part of a party or event revolves around deciding how to word the invitations so that you clarify details and minimize questions.

To make things easy, begin by stating the occasion or event, including date, time, location, and purpose. And don't forget to mention whether spouses, children, or other family members are invited. Either throw open the gates enthusiastically or limit surprises—but do so tactfully.

> *"Children will have other activities provided."*
>
> *"Only members of the immediate family are invited for this occasion."*
>
> *"Our accommodations have limited our guest list to include only those who…"*
>
> *"If you plan to bring a guest, please let us know by calling…"*
>
> *"Come and bring your guest."*
>
> *"If you know of others who may be interested, invite them to attend with you."*

Overview scheduling for any planned activities. These details will help guests understand about the appropriateness of arriving early or late or other schedule conflicts during the event.

State the appropriate dress, if that is not obvious from the occasion, activities, and site.

> *"Business attire is required."*
>
> *"All our guests will probably be coming straight from work, so your professional attire is appropriate."*

"Business casual is the appropriate dress."

"Beachwear is the order of the day."

"Wear something comfortable for working and walking."

"We'll be outdoors, so dress accordingly."

"Dress in your partying clothes."

"Festive attire is appropriate."

Ask for a response by a certain date so that you aren't left with indecision about food and space logistics. Or, if a response isn't necessary, say so.

State tactfully preferences or appropriateness of gifts. No mention of gifts leaves readers to do what they wish, or nothing at all. If you want to leave the giving decision open, avoid any mention of gifts.

"Gag gifts, OK."

"Please send your love in lieu of gifts."

"No gifts, please."

"Mary has asked that no gifts be sent. Please send any donations to…"

"Tara's planning a color scheme of green and plum in the bath and kitchen."

Having this arduous chore of composing the invitations behind you, enjoy the party!

FORMAL

• BABY SHOWER •

It's a girl—or at least that's what the doctors say at this point.

You're invited to a baby shower for Melissa Edwards.
May 5 from 12 to 2 p.m.

Carter's Tea Room
455 Oak Lawn

RSVP by May 2 (499-3434).
We're planning a light lunch.

• BIRTHDAY PARTY •

You are invited to a party honoring Mattie Matthews on her ninetieth birthday, December 1. Mattie has gone from horses to jets, from no phones to mobile phones, from inkwells to computer chips. What a fantastic day to gather around and hear her varied experiences with life!

The party will be at the Carver Room, in the Hartford Civic Center. Please stop by sometime between the hours of 2 and 5 p.m. to express your best wishes to Mattie. No gifts, please.

• BRIDAL SHOWER •

You are invited to a bridal shower honoring Laura Newman, on January 14, from 4 to 6 in the afternoon. Please reply to Mary Cox (344-5898) if you will be able to join us after work for cocktails and hors d'oeuvres.

The bride is registered at the following stores: Dillard's, Foley's, The Kit and Kaboodle, and Bradford's.

Big Tip 1: Since Laura has experienced apartment living for several years, she has the necessities in the kitchen. But the extras, well, that's where you come in.

Big Tip 2: Colors throughout the apartment are burgundy and forest green.

• CHRISTENING •

Christening of our daughter
Sheree Lynn Stewart

Sunday, February 6, at 6 p.m.

St. Thomas Episcopal Church
388 Foster Road
Wyatt, Iowa

RSVP for the dinner following: (123) 333-4894

• WEDDING AT CLUB •

Friends and Family

You are invited to join us in celebrating our love, on Saturday, November 6, at the Grand Kapinski Hotel, in the Love Nest, 39393 Los Alamos Freeway, Los Angeles.

We ask that you, our very closest friends, be with us as we say our wedding vows at 7 p.m., and then join us at the reception following the ceremony. Your being with us on this occasion will complete our special day.

Regrets only: 459-0022

• WEDDING AT HOME •

We are pleased to invite you to the wedding of our daughter, Alicia Kay McGown, to Mark Hanson on Friday, May 7, at 8 p.m. in our home at 5782 Miramar Road in the Southlake Vista.

After the couple exchanges vows, we invite you to join us for a buffet dinner honoring our children. Please respond (564-8866) by April 15 if you will be able to attend.

• CANCELLATION OF INVITATION •

Mr. and Mrs. Len Everett
are recalling their invitations to the
marriage of their daughter
Carrie Frazier
to
Spencer Ludlow

The wedding will not take place
because of Spencer's
prolonged illness.

Note: If the reason is not meant for common knowledge—if it's something other than military obligations, illness, or death in the family—you may simply wish to end with this generic explanation: "The wedding will not take place."

INFORMAL

• ANNIVERSARY PARTY—FOR FRIENDS •

Maria and Jose Gonzales
are celebrating their
Golden Wedding Anniversary
on February 1, at 7 p.m.

Please join us in our home for a buffet dinner
to congratulate the happy couple.

Given by Denise and Sandy Baxter
973 Blair Lane
(301) 494-9949

RSVP by January 21 please.

• ANNIVERSARY PARTY—YOUR OWN ANNIVERSARY •

We're celebrating our twenty-fifth wedding anniversary
and hope you'll join us.

What? Sit-down dinner, followed by dancing
When? June 22 at 8 p.m.
Where? Harvey Hotel at 848 Lamar Boulevard
Why? We appreciate our friends and family.

Eric and Susan Johnson

RSVP by June 1 (card enclosed)

• BIRTHDAY PARTY—NO GIFTS •

It's the big 50 for Gordie McWilliams.
He'll never have a good night's sleep again.

Dress casual and be prepared to party
on March 31 at 7 p.m.
Rinehart's Restaurant at Central and Bowen Expressway

RSVP: 444-8980 by March 28

No gifts; just come eat our grub.

• BIRTHDAY PARTY—SURPRISE •

It's a surprise!

Todd Matthews turns into superman on his twenty-first birthday.

Come party with us!
January 14 at 8 p.m.
Backyard Barbecue

Fran and Frances McIntire's Place
292 Westway

No need to call; for those who don't show up, we'll send out a posse.
Gag gifts only.

• HOLIDAY SEASON •

Join us for a preholiday party to meet and greet your neighbors!

Dessert and Drinks

November 29 from 8 to 11 p.m.

Harry and Cinda Cosco's Home
4899 Casablanca Boulevard

Dress: Festive

• PARTY FOR VISITING FRIEND OR GUEST •

It's a party for our summer houseguest!
Our niece, Melissa Parks

Saturday, June 1, at 7 p.m.

Stop by to meet and charm Melissa, and then say hello to friends and neighbors you haven't seen in a while. You might be surprised at what they've been up to lately!

Dress: Casual

• SOCIAL CLUB MIXER •

Try us; you'll like us.

Chapter Mixer, sponsored by the Laketon Literary Club
Date: August 7
Time: 7 to 8:30 p.m.

Program: Roundtables with local authors
Chilton Library, Conference Room B
Foster at Central Expressway
Reception following at Ernie's Eatery, across the street.

• THEME PARTIES •

1980s

It's a 1980s Rerun

Party Hearty!

Friday, June 5 at 7 p.m.

Jill and Damon McWhorter's Place
5900 Dill Drive, Apartment C

Dress as you did in high school: casual and comfortable.
Bring a snack tray, bowl, or basket with your favorite goodies.

• THEME PARTIES •

Movie Madness

Movie Madness after the Holidays

January 6 at 7 p.m.

We're planning to have videos of all the classics playing in the background.

Come prepared to laugh and cry with the stars!

Dress: Clothes, any flavor will do
Bring a dessert and a beverage

Sponsored by the Mavericks' Club

• THEME PARTIES •

Romeo and Juliet

Romeo and Juliet Party
Come in costume as a famous, romantic twosome

February 14 at 8 p.m.

Wyndham Hotel, Wedgewood Room
3833 Lovers Lane

Pay at the door: $45 per couple for all the
food, music, and fun you can enjoy

RSVP: Call Mary Watson (433-5858)
or Cathy Garcia (454-4444)
by February 12

JOB REFERENCES AND INTRODUCTIONS

On occasion, you will be the go-between for friends, relatives, and associates. They'll need character references, nominations, and introductions. Don't let the task of phrasing a good letter keep you from helping someone in these situations. Writing a reference letter puts your friend or family member in the limelight and banks a favor for your own future.

When you can enthusiastically introduce or refer someone, get to the point immediately; introduce or recommend the person in the first sentence or paragraph. Then overview the person's association or acquaintance with you: In what capacity did or do you know this person? How have you become aware of his or her skills, talent, character traits, or success?

> "I've known Johnny for years as a fellow swimmer on the neighborhood team."

> "Johnny's children and mine have grown up together. We've lived in the same neighborhood for almost 16 years."

> "Over the years I've served with Johnny on several boards in which I've noted his financial savvy about..."

> "Sara's creative talents often came in handy in PTA fund-raising projects."

> "Sara has been a faithful attendee of my congregation for almost 10 years, and during that time, I've often called upon her to..."

Be as specific as possible about the person's skills, attitudes, and accomplishments. If possible, relate them to benefits for the group or association to which you're making the referral, recommendation, or introduction.

> *"Cary's flexible attitude in fast-changing environments would certainly come in handy in dealing with your membership."*
>
> *"Because your organization depends on the fund-raising efforts of its members, I know that Ming would be willing to access her network of friends to tap into their resources and energies."*

Express confidence that any future association between the reader and your friend or family member will be mutually rewarding.

> *"We know you'll profit from any conversations; you are both so well versed on the subject."*
>
> *"We think you'll really hit it off together."*
>
> *"Any association between you two can only be mutually rewarding."*
>
> *"I'm very confident that Michael will become an outstanding student at your university."*
>
> *"Dominick, if he should win this award, will bring great distinction to your organization for having recognized his talents."*

When writing reference letters, you have a unique chance to do a favor for two people with only a few strokes on your keyboard.

• SUPPLYING REFERENCE FOR STUDENT •

To Whom It May Concern:

I highly recommend Andrea Goldstein for summer employment in your organization. As a freshman and sophomore, Andrea worked for me as assistant in my law practice. She performed various clerical duties, including word processing, copying and collating, filing, courier services, and errands to clients' and vendors' offices.

My staff and I found her to be extremely mature in dealing with clients and flexible in changing priorities almost daily. We were pleased with her word processing speed and accuracy in customizing our tedious technical forms and documents. In addition, she was punctual and had no absences during the two summers with us—quite a record, considering the schedules of today's busy teens.

Regrettably, Andrea will not be continuing employment with us this coming summer, because we have moved our law practice out of the neighborhood where she attends high school. The extra 15 minutes in commuter traffic makes the move for her impractical.

If Andrea accepts a position with your firm, we think you'll be very pleased with her work and attitude.

Yours truly,

• SUPPLYING REFERENCE FOR EMPLOYEE •

To Prospective Employers:

Danette Schronk has provided cleaning and nanny services for our family for the past 4 years, and we have been very pleased with her work. We became acquainted with Danette while we were visiting a friend in Germany. Later, when we learned that she wanted to come to the United States, we quickly invited her to work for us and helped her get the necessary legal clearances to do so.

Danette's job responsibilities with us have included the typical household duties, cooking for our family of four, and caring for two preschool children. Danette speaks impeccable English, demonstrates a congenial attitude toward all in our family, and understands the importance of giving loving attention and discipline to the children—not to mention her considerable culinary talents!

We were very disappointed when Danette told us of her plans to enroll as a full-time university student and seek only part-time employment. Had we not needed someone full time to care for our preschoolers, we would still insist on having Danette with us.

Any family who employs Danette in the future will find her personable, efficient, and honest.

• Supplying Character Reference for Friend •

Dear Mr. Lee:

Garrett Truman, a good friend of mine, has recently left his job at Atwood Engineering to start his own consulting practice, specializing in computer training for small businesses. His 16 years inside a major corporation that manufactures and installs various telecommunications systems around the country have certainly prepared him for the new venture.

What's lacking is a solid list of prospects needing his services. That's where I come in. I offered to contact a few friends of mine who have their own professional practice or small business and need his services to train themselves or staff in the array of new software packages flooding the market.

Garrett's previous employer and satisfied customers can attest to his technical skills. I myself know this man's attitude and character. He is a creative individual with the perseverance to get the job done—whatever that takes. He's patient with those who suffer from computer phobia (personal experience here), and can quickly grasp the business applications of your operation and identify the must-know from the nice-to-know tasks that you or your staff need to perform on the computer. That translates into increased productivity sooner rather than later.

Should you have need of computer training at the moment, I encourage you to give Garrett a call at (415) 686-3939. I think you'll find it a mutually rewarding relationship. Best wishes for your own continued success.

Sincerely,

• SUPPLYING REFERENCE FOR FRIEND FOR CLUB MEMBERSHIP •

Dear Committee Members:

With this letter, I am recommending Cameron Baker for membership in the Brighton Club. Cameron and his family moved to Bynum 3 months ago from Chicago, where he served as hospital administrator for the Medicare clinic system. His wife had her own practice there as a pediatrician in Napersville. Currently, both of them are pursuing the same careers here. She has established her pediatric practice with the Methodist Hospital, and Cameron has assumed a similar administrative position with the same hospital.

Our family's association with this family began more than 10 years ago, when our sons played on the same Little League team in Chicago. We struck up a casual acquaintance and then a closer friendship as we served on several corporate boards together.

I find Cameron and his wife to be dedicated professionals in their medical careers, capable leaders in the community, and of high moral character. Our organization could profit immeasurably from their membership, talents, and insight.

Sincerely,

• INTRODUCING RELATIVE TO EMPLOYER •

Dear Bonnie:

My brother, Jeffrey, has just returned to Dayton to seek employment so that he can be near our elderly parents. When he told me that he wanted to continue his long sales career with a premium organization—selling a service that he believes has lasting value for people—I immediately thought of you.

Jeffrey has sold both products and services in the past 20 years: telephone systems, copiers, software, training, and public relations services. And, I might add, he has done very well at it, having been recognized by two previous employers for exceeding revenue goals and landing in the Top 10 Percent Club at their respective organizations.

If you need a self-starter with a track record, you may want to set up an interview with Jeffrey. He'll be moving here in July, but he can fly in for an interview at your convenience. Let me know if you think you could benefit from meeting Jeffrey to see if there's a match in temperament and philosophy.

I always love being a matchmaker—especially when the relationship could be so rewarding for both parties involved. If I don't hear from you, I'll assume you have no positions available at the present. In any case, do stay in touch. Hope you're having another great year at FlexMart.

Cordially,

• NOMINATING CANDIDATE FOR AWARD •

Dear Committee:

With this letter, I am nominating Tommye Nell Bradford as Citizen of the Year at Summersville.

For 15 years, Tommye Nell has devoted countless hours to community projects. But this year, her efforts have been unsurpassed and invaluable to our citizens. As chair of the United Way campaign for the city, she raised more than $14 million, representing a 22 percent increase over any previous year. That in itself is a gargantuan achievement.

But Tommye's efforts have also extended to service on the board of directors for Habitat for the Homeless, Snyder's Mission, and the Glasgow Art Museum. Through her countless efforts on these boards, she has indeed created a caring and nurturing environment in our community. We owe much of our heritage to similar efforts of hers in the 20 years since she and her family have made their home here.

The Citizen of the Year award could go to no finer resident than Tommye Nell Bradford. It's time Summersville offered a sincere thank-you for her many contributions.

Sincerely,

• RECOMMENDING GUEST SPEAKER •

Dear Members:

Jessica Dalton is the epitome of a professional speaker extraordinaire: expertise established through years of solid research, a dynamic delivery style, and ethical standards so important to today's audiences.

I'd like to recommend Jessica to you as a valuable resource for your next annual meeting. I've known Jessica for about 3 years through my employer, Frito-Lay. We engaged her to deliver various concurrent sessions at our national sales meetings, and our attendees found her to be always prepared, on target with the latest research, and focused with practical marketing strategies for immediate use. We had more positive comments on her sessions than on all the others combined.

If you'd like to know more about the results we were able to achieve with the information Jessica provided, give me a call to review our audience profiles and evaluations in greater detail.

Although I've left Frito-Lay, Jessica is still traveling the country addressing the top corporations in the area of her expertise: marketing in the global economy. If you ever find yourself looking for an expert on that topic, you could not find someone more qualified or more effective in moving audiences into action than Jessica Dalton.

Sincerely,

• DECLINING TO SUPPLY CHARACTER REFERENCE •

Dear Jeremy,

I received your message yesterday about using my name as a reference in your job search.

Through our association at the club, as you probably recall, we did not often agree on our budgeting priorities and membership goals. Therefore, I'm afraid any comments I might pass on to a prospective employer would be biased by those difficulties at the club. So I've concluded that it might be in your best interest for me not to comment on those differing views.

I wish you success in finding a suitable job.

Sincerely,

LETTERS TO YOUNG CHILDREN

On first blush, you might consider writing a note or letter to a child an easy task. But writing that does not sound condescending or silly and that demonstrates to a child that you understand his or her world takes a little thought.

Generally, you are safe to start by complimenting the child specifically for behavior and action. Instead of "You've been a very good student," try:

> *"Your mother tells me that you've earned all A's this semester. And I imagine that's not easy with the two science courses you're taking."*

Make the child feel special by mentioning details (names, occasions, toys or games, comments, feelings) that are special to him or her personally. Empathize with and accept feelings he or she has expressed in the past.

> *"I know that you must have been afraid to try something like this."*
>
> *"I know that you have spent hours working on the project."*
>
> *"Most children feel very disappointed when something like this happens."*

Above all, express your love and appreciation, focusing on the child's concerns, not your own.

• CONGRATULATIONS ON SCHOOLWORK •

Dear Juan,

Thank you for writing to me and sending your grades for this year. I'm always so concerned that you're studying hard. And it certainly looks like you are. Your math grades came up two points from last time. That must mean you understand your fractions now well enough to do those word problems. I still have difficulty with fractions myself from time to time when I'm drawing those house plans.

Thanks for keeping me updated. I'll expect more good news next semester.

Love,

• Happy Birthday •

Tommy,

Happy birthday on your seventh big event. I understand that you're planning a great camping trip for the weekend to celebrate with your friends. Be sure not to forget to eat an extra hot dog for me—with lots of mustard, just the way you and I like them.

I'm proud of the kind and bright young man you've become.

With love,

• PLEASE VISIT •

Dear Mark and Leanne,

Would you be able to spend a few days with us in Seattle while you're out of school for the holidays? We'd love to send you airline tickets if your mother thinks you can arrange to come. If you can be with us, here are some suggestions for what we might do. (*fill in details.*)

What do you say? I'll be waiting to have you call me after you and your mom have had time to look at your schedules.

Love,

• PLEASE COME AGAIN •

Phillip,

I can hardly believe you've already come and gone. Your grandaddy is still adding snow patches to Frosty in the backyard. His hat is lopsided, but otherwise, he's still in fairly good shape.

The most fun we had with you was tucking you into bed each night and reading those new stories we bought last weekend. Do you still remember what happened to Donald, the Muckety-Muck?

Please ask your dad to call us on the weekend to let us know if you need a refill on the books.

With love,

• THANK YOU FOR GIFT •

Dear Brianna:

How sweet of you to send the pictures to me. I really like the one you took on top of the mountain. Where was that? How high were you?

You were pretty sharp to remind your folks to get double prints made for me. Let's you and me keep working with those two and we'll have them remembering to do that every time! Thank you for including me in your vacation.

Love,

MEDIA: ISSUES, CONCERNS, POSITIONS

You need to deal with the media—to conduct your life and fulfill community obligations—in various frames of minds, from elation for coverage about hazardous situations to anger about offensive programming. Your purpose must determine your tone.

To request services, begin by stating the action you want—that's your message.

> *"Please retract immediately the statement that..."*
>
> *"I'd like to request equal time to present the opposing views about..."*
>
> *"Please place my ad in Sunday's paper in the section called..."*

Answer the 6 W's questions for public service announcements: what, who, when, why, where, how, how much. Finally, provide contact information for further questions.

On those occasions when you intend to show support, express your appreciation for the media's position on an issue, ad, or controversy or for media sponsorship of decent, beneficial programming.

> *"We wholeheartedly embrace and welcome the new program you've decided to air about..."*
>
> *"I commend you for taking a strong stand against..."*
>
> *"I read with great appreciation your editorial about..."*
>
> *"Thank you for calling attention to the often overlooked issue of..."*

Then add your own reasons for agreeing with the media's position or action.

Commend the media for shedding light on any complex issue and spending time and effort in the investigative process, and thank them for bringing issues or problems to the public's attention.

> *"I'm sure the background facts you printed were not easy to dislodge from such protective agencies."*
>
> *"I appreciate the fact that your reporter made several trips overseas to get to the bottom of this matter."*
>
> *"This situation is complex and your investigation shows that you did more than a cursory review."*
>
> *"You have done us all a big favor."*

When you object to the media's position or action, speak up. That's your right as a citizen. Identify yourself so as to add authority to what you say:

> *"As a well-known citizen frequently speaking to civic groups about…"*
>
> *"As a taxpayer who contributes over $X in property taxes each year…"*
>
> *"As a principal of the high school who intends to advise teachers and students against the policy stated in the media…"*
>
> *"As an active voter and grass-roots supporter during election campaigns…"*

Give your reasons for the disagreement or objection, pointing out any erroneous information and giving your sources of information in support of your position. Take care to point out the ill-will, harm, or other negative ramifications of the media's position and urge them to reverse their position or action or broadcast a retraction.

Finally, don't forget the positives within the power of the media. If you know of an issue that needs coverage or a problem to be resolved, be proactive in contacting the media and suggesting a story. They need more, not fewer, concerned citizens.

• PRESS RELEASE—PUBLIC SERVICE ANNOUNCEMENT •

For Immediate Release

As publicity director of the Bonnham Supplies for Students Fund this summer, I'm making you aware of a drive to collect used school supplies for the needy children in our local districts. We'd appreciate it if you would announce this drive—its purpose, the collection points, and the distribution center—during your after-school driving time.

> Join us in our Bonnham Supplies for Students Drive. Many children find that they outgrow or stop using their old school jackets, sweats and warm-up suits, notebooks, and supplementary reading texts as they complete various courses. We're asking parents and students to donate these used-but-still-good items to our collection for use by other children.
>
> I've listed below the various collection points around the city. We will be sending a truck to pick up these items and bring them to a central location on Monday evenings. Those students and their parents needing such items will be allowed to make their selections from our central headquarters office at 478 Davis Street.
>
> Collection point: Your neighborhood fire station
>
> For further information, listeners may call 123-4567.

Thank you for your help in spreading the news about these available school supplies for needy families.

For further information: Contact publicity director Lyle Raymond at 433-4345.

• PLACING CLASSIFIED ADVERTISEMENT •

Dear Manager of the Classified Ads:

Please place the following ad in the Sunday edition of the paper in the section "Used Cars":

1996 Buick Regal: 12,000 miles. Excellent condition. $17,000.

Call 344-9987 after 7 p.m. or any time on weekends.

I've enclosed a check for $35 for the ad to run Sunday only. I understand that if I want to continue the ad on Sundays, I can phone by noon the following Friday and run it again for only $30 on subsequent insertions.

My work number for any questions you may have is 445-9982.

Sincerely,

• PLACING PROFESSIONAL ANNOUNCEMENT •

Dear Editor:

Please place the following announcement in your "Bulletin Board" section of the business journal supplement that runs every Tuesday:

> The American Society for Training and Development will hold its monthly meeting, February 16, at a new location: the Hilton at Lamar Avenue. The meeting will begin with cocktails and registration at 6:00, followed by dinner at 6:30 and a speaker at 7:30. Charge for members is $25; for nonmembers, $35. For registration, call 444-6666 by noon of the meeting day.

Thank you for this placement.

Sincerely,

• PROTESTING CANCELLATION OF COLUMN/COMIC STRIP/PROGRAM/SERIES •

Dear Ms. McCormick:

I am very disappointed about your decision to cancel Mike Hardy's column on employment and job searches. Isn't it bad enough that so many of your readers have been "canceled" from their jobs and employers? Must you add to our dilemma by eliminating a very good source of job search tips and strategies?

Won't you please reconsider your decision to cancel Hardy's column?

Certainly, you are aware that the employment rate in this state stands at 8.5 percent, according to a front-page story your paper ran 2 weeks ago. And many job seekers cannot afford to buy all the job-hunting books from their local bookstores. Hardy's column on current trends in résumé writing, interviewing techniques, and compensation fills a big gap in the knowledge base of so many who've been with one employer for much too long to understand the complexities of the job market.

Not only does the column speak to the needs of the unemployed, but it also serves to make large corporations aware of the recruitment tactics and compensation packages offered by their competitors. My wife, a human resources specialist for a large oil company, also finds the columns up to date in their recommendations and information about trends in the HR field.

No, Mike Hardy is not my brother-in-law. But I am a devoted fan, and I do hope you'll continue to carry his column in the weeks to come. I need to spend my time finding a new job, not a new newspaper.

Sincerely,

• Objecting to Cartoon/Ad/Program/Series •

Dear Mr. Phillips:

I strongly object to the new 30-minute sitcom *Free for All.* Although the basic premise of the show holds promise, the situations and dialogues of the characters constantly attack marriage and religious commitments. I find these opinions outside the mainstream of American lives and morally objectionable.

Worse, this program is aired in prime time, when impressionable children and teens are most likely to be watching.

I strongly urge you to drop this program from your lineup and return to programs that strengthen rather destroy the moral fabric of our country. By a copy of this letter, I'm also making my opinion known to the corporate advertisers sponsoring this program.

Sincerely,

• COMPLAINING TO PROGRAM'S SPONSOR •

Dear Ms. Susamm:

I was shocked to see your Gotchas, one of my favorite snacks, advertised during the broadcast of *Free for All*. My family and friends strongly urge you to reconsider that sponsorship and advertising decision.

We find the program particularly objectionable because it continually pokes fun at marriage and religious commitments. And we're surprised that a reputable company such as yours, which aims to reach the family market, would become associated with such a program.

If you cancel this advertisement and can persuade other sponsors to do the same, perhaps the TV network will be forced to drop the sitcom. The typical American household will certainly be the winner in that scenario.

We strongly urge you to consider this request so that we can continue to buy Gotchas in good conscience.

Sincerely,

• SUPPORTING EDITORIAL POSITION •

Dear Mr. Tan:

We applaud your position to repeal Legislative Bill H3889, commonly known as the Sit-Down Tax, and we thank you for highlighting this important issue in recent editorials.

Two years ago when they passed this bill, our state representatives focused on the least effective and most objectionable way to raise revenue. The intent of the bill was to rid our streets of the homeless, but the real effect of this bill has been to drive the homeless into shelters that are overcrowded and now dangerous themselves.

Thank you for investigating the far-reaching results of this law and bringing it to the attention of our lawmakers and our citizens.

Sincerely,

• CANCELING SUBSCRIPTION OVER POLITICAL ISSUE •

Dear Editor:

Please cancel our subscription to your newspaper, effective immediately. Although we've been subscribers for more than 10 years, this past Sunday's editorial in support of redrawing our school district lines angered us to the point of taking drastic action.

My family and I, as well as those families I've spoken with in the community of Lakeview, oppose such gerrymandering of the school district on moral grounds. From the gist of the editorial, it is clear that the very few, but vocal, proponents of that action have racial discrimination as their primary purpose. That observation becomes very evident as one reviews the proposed new district lines, as mapped and distributed by the Lakeview Board of Education.

We believe that children need personal interactions with people of all races and economic conditions to teach them appreciation for the various cultures represented in our society. To redraw the lines solely to ensure that the races are kept separate smacks of the 1950s.

Frankly, we are shocked that your newspaper has taken such a stand. We hope you'll reconsider this position and take to higher moral ground with those readers who look to your newspaper as their only source of information.

Sincerely,

• SUGGESTING STORY FOR COVERAGE •

Dear Ms. Sanchez:

I frequently travel out of the Dallas–Fort Worth airport and have few, if any, options for transportation home to the nearby city of Euless. It seems that taxi drivers think the minimum fare of $14 out of the airport is "peanuts" and often drive off and leave passengers standing on the curb when they discover their destination.

I, as well as several other Euless and Grapevine passengers, have been harassed, cursed, and detained by cabbies waiting on another, more profitable passenger to join me before they would agree to drive me to my destination. And after the shuttle services stop running at night, late travelers have no other options to get to their nearby homes.

When I've phoned and written the various cab companies (letters enclosed) to complain about their drivers refusing to accept a passenger going to Euless, the company officials all insist that their drivers are "required" to take passengers anywhere as long as they collect the minimum fare. But the company officials' statements to that effect do not ensure that their drivers comply. To my knowledge, they've taken no action to ensure that their cabs provide service to Euless.

I've also written our mayor (as suggested by one cabby) to petition the city to raise the minimum fare to ensure service to the community. To date, the mayor's office has not responded and no action has been taken.

I and my fellow midcities frequent flyers urge your help in investigating this frustrating, not to mention unsafe, situation.

Sincerely,

OPINIONS AND POLITICS

Only those who communicate with their elected leaders have the right to complain when events don't suit them. Change comes from persistent, clear communication from the communities that cast the ballots.

So to grab attention and get action, describe yourself as a voter, supporter of the cause, taxpayer, citizen, business executive, organizational spokesperson, industry leader, or some other label that underscores your leadership role and intention to influence others.

> *"I'm writing because, as a teacher and coach, I see every day in the classroom and on the court and hear from parents that..."*
>
> *"I'll be addressing those leaders in my industry at an upcoming seminar and want to be able to summarize your position about..."*
>
> *"As I travel around the state speaking on community college campuses, I often discover that..."*

Refer to the political issue or legislative bill by its popular title or by a number or referendum. Use any such number or title in a reference line above the body of the letter as well as in the body of the letter itself.

State specifically the action you want from your readers. Do you want them to vote for or against? Do you want money or an investigation? Do you want them to fund or stop funding a cause? Do you want them to introduce a bill or kill it in committee? Then elaborate on the reason behind your opinion or request for action.

When your expertise will grab attention, use it. Expand on your credentials or experience with regard to a position on a technical issue.

"As a biochemist with 15 years of research in..."

"As a parent of four teenagers in our school system..."

"As a volunteer having served in a number of positions in this industry during the past 20 years..."

Expand your clout by letting readers know of your intention to make others aware of their position, reply, or action (or inaction).

"I will be publishing your statement in a monthly letter to our members."

"We will be including your views in announcements we send home with our students."

"I plan to incorporate your response in my speech to the officers of our group."

Remember that politicians focus only on one issue at a time. So focus your comments on only the most pressing matter; save other issues and problems until later letters.

Finally, nothing motivates people for a repeat performance more than recognition and gratitude. When you appreciate a politician's or community leader's efforts or position, say so and be specific about the commendation. Performance rewarded is performance repeated.

• TO THE PRESIDENT—SUPPORTING BILL OR ISSUE •

The Honorable President of the United States
1600 Pennsylvania Avenue
Washington, DC 20510

Dear Mr. President:

Building a strong armed forces to ensure peace in the new millennium in a global marketplace will be the primary challenge of your presidency. You have campaigned hard on this issue and won my support. That support this past year took the form of monetary contributions to your campaign fund, attendance at political rallies, telephone canvassing, and public speeches as a member of my local city council.

A strong armed forces means that our country can respond to aggressors who determine that they will unexpectedly invade their smaller neighbors and rape the natural resources of the land. A strong armed forces means that our country can protect its own citizens who wish to live or travel abroad. A strong armed forces means that foreign demagogues will consider the cost and loss before violating human rights of their own citizens. Finally, a strong armed forces ensures that our economic interests are protected around the world.

I urge you not to let this issue take a back seat to other domestic problems and issues put before you by special-interests groups. My family, coworkers, and civic colleagues will be keenly aware of your leadership as the military funding bills are presented to Congress during your new term.

Thank you for your past years of service to the country.

Respectfully,

• TO LEGISLATOR—CONGRATULATING ON PASSAGE OF LEGISLATION •

The Honorable Leroy Battwann
Texas Senate
Austin, TX 78710

RE: S7898-88

Dear Senator Battwann:

We want to offer our congratulations on the successful passage of the recent tax bill to raise revenue to improve our state highway system. When things don't go well, I'm sure you hear from your constituents loudly and frequently, so we wanted you to know that we are pleased with your sponsorship of the bill and your skillful guiding of that bill through the Senate.

With the outspoken special-interest groups crying "foul" about the speed limits, you faced incredible odds against getting your message to the citizenry. The effort you spent in calling press conferences, from which excerpts were aired in prime time, certainly helped voters understand the real issues.

Keep up the good work on the behalf of all the citizens in our state.

Sincerely,

• TO LEGISLATOR—OPPOSING BILL OR ISSUE •

The Honorable Karen Fulton
U.S. Senate
Washington, DC 20510

RE: HR 98989

Dear Senator Fulton:

I strongly oppose the idea of federally funded day-care centers built in corporate environments around the country. If the bill now before Congress (HR 98989) passes, this day-care system will cost taxpayers an estimated $8 billion annually, according to a recent article in *Time* magazine.

Am I antifamily? Am I anti-working mothers? No. I'm a single parent with two small children of day-care age. Despite the "convenience" of dropping my children off every day as I go to my management job with a large oil company, I fear the government intrusion into our free-enterprise system. If the government built such day-care centers on corporate sites with the proposed tax credits, the next round of regulations would involve the government telling the corporations how much tuition to charge their employees and then helping them formulate "policies" about sickness, discipline problems, and "bridging" from one corporation's day care to another after termination of employment. In other words, the intrusion and complexities will grow.

Would you please let me know how you plan to vote on this issue? As a manager of the human resources function in our corporation, I will be updating our employees about your comments and voting record on this important legislation.

Sincerely,

• TO LEGISLATOR—PROTESTING TAX INCREASE •

RE: State Senate Bill S9399932

The Honorable Justin P. O'Leary

Dear Senator O'Leary:

As a long-time worker in your past election campaigns, I strongly protest the proposed 3-cents-a-gallon increase in gasoline taxes now under consideration in our state legislature.

This tax unfairly penalizes commuters who live in small towns and must drive to the larger metropolitan areas for work. Instead, I propose an increase in the luxury tax to raise the revenues we need in the state. Such a tax would place the burden of the tax on those who can best afford it, as evidenced by their purchase of luxury cars, furs, and recreational vehicles.

I urge you to vote no when this bill comes up on the senate floor. Please respond to me about you views on this tax issue.

Sincerely,

• To Legislator—Asking for Help •

The Honorable Felix D'Amato
U.S. House of Representatives
Washington, DC 20510

Dear Congressman D'Amato:

Congratulations on you recent reelection. You have an excellent record of supporting the concerns and needs of the elderly. That's why, during your campaign, three of my letters to the editors of our local newspapers were published, stating why I urged voters to support you in your reelection efforts.

Now that you've achieved your mission, I'd like to ask your help in achieving mine. My 70-year-old mother (diabetic, confined to a wheelchair, and a recent widow) is having great difficulty in finding an apartment on the HUD-approved and subsidized list. It seems that all apartment complexes in our city of Edmonton have waiting lists, and their managers estimate the wait for an apartment to be 6 to 12 months.

Specifically, the Elrod Apartment Complex, located at 477 Center Street and managed by Alfred Sloan, is refusing even to add my mother's name to the list because of the long wait. I might add that Mr. Sloan has been rather surly, stating blatantly that he tries not to rent to anyone who needs wheelchair access to central areas because of the "traffic" problems on the sidewalks.

I'd appreciate your help in providing a list of all HUD-approved housing available in our city and investigating the Elrod Apartment Complex specifically to ensure that this manager complies with government regulations with regard to unbiased award of the apartments to future tenants.

(Continued)

Enclosed is my mother's application, including the financial information required.

Please respond to me at the above address and phone number. Thank you for any help you can provide in finding my mother HUD housing.

Sincerely,

• TO LEGISLATOR—SUPPORTING CAMPAIGN FOR OFFICE •

Dear Mr. McCormick:

We are behind your bid for Congress 100 percent. Thank you for your stand on returning order to our classrooms by giving teachers and school administrators the laws they need to earn the respect of their students and to create a learning environment.

Second, we believe in your stand against forbidding public prayer in the classroom and think your pro-life position for the unborn will help rebuild the moral fiber in our marriages and family. We strongly reaffirm the separation of church and state, and we value human life in all forms.

Would you send us your literature summarizing your stand on these issues, as well as your position on other issues facing our country? We plan to duplicate and distribute copies of your campaign platform to our church groups and to the 1100 employees in our small business.

If you need additional volunteers for telephone canvassing in the evening hours, please have someone on your staff contact us. We look forward to working with you at the grassroots level to change the future of our country.

Sincerely,

• TO LEGISLATOR—REGRETTING ELECTION DEFEAT •

Dear Mayor Robertson:

We are deeply disappointed by last week's vote and regret that you will not be serving another term as our mayor. As you make your plans to leave office, we want you to know how much we have appreciated your leadership.

Specifically, we want to highlight the many accomplishments of your past two terms: the expansion of our park system, the revenue-generating arrangement for summer youth activities, the excellent condition of our once pothole-filled streets. The most significant accomplishments have to do with your positioning the city to attract major corporations here. As a result of your work, we've seen numerous corporations (Walmart, JCPenney, Honeywell, and Steinmart) move into our city limits, thereby significantly expanding our tax base.

The citizens of Harrisburg owe you a great deal. Thank you for your service to the community these past 8 years.

Sincerely,

• TO LEGISLATOR—SUPPORTING BOND ISSUE •

Dear Representative Corona:

As a well-informed citizen and resident of Minnesota, I favor the construction of the TGV train between Foster and Mackentown. No doubt the completion of such an undertaking will save Minnesota residents an infinite sum of money in the long run, not to mention prevent an inestimable number of highway fatalities, as well as aid the protection of the environment.

I am confident that you will continue to champion the construction of the TGV despite others who may shortsightedly protest it. I would like to congratulate you for standing firm so far, and encourage you to persist in your efforts.

I, myself, am well acquainted with traveling Highway 287 between Foster and Mackentown on a regular basis. My family lives in Foster, and when I was a college student at the University of Mackentown, it seemed as though I was always driving that expanse of road. I saw countless accidents and was even in a minor one myself. I now occasionally travel this route on business, and in addition to my personal safety, I have become increasingly concerned with the environmental damage caused by the heavy traffic that frequents this highway.

The TGV could eradicate these problems, which will only worsen as Minnesota's population grows. Support this objective, and you will win my reelection vote.

Your loyal constituent,

PARENTAL CONCERNS

Rearing children means having to say you're sorry, having to express appreciation, having to offer explanations, and having to request action by or information from schools, sports clubs, and governmental agencies.

In these various situations, you'll need to summarize your commendation, complaint, request, or permission in a sentence or two at the beginning of the letter.

> *"I'm writing to suggest an investigation into why…"*
>
> *"I need some information about your plans to…"*
>
> *"I want to commend you on the way in which you have…"*
>
> *"We're having difficulty understanding your recent policy to…"*

Be specific when requesting corrective action or resolution of a problem.

Remember to use your child's full legal name in any reference, especially if the last name differs from yours. For formal matters, include this information in a reference line. Also include dates of past or future attendance at the school and any other identifying information for quick recall and association, such as "enrolled in Mr. Turner's ESL classes in the after-school program."

And be sure to alert the school or religious officials to any potential danger and any precautions you are suggesting in relation to your child's safety or health.

In sensitive situations, make it clear whether the information you are supplying should be kept confidentially from your child. Or state whether your child has been given the same explanation or instructions as you are giving the school or religious organization. For example:

> *"I have not told Susan that I was writing you about her condition."*
>
> *"I'd appreciate it if you'd not mention to Susan our discussion."*
>
> *"Thank you for being discreet in any action you take so that others will not isolate Susan for this condition."*
>
> *"You may feel free to discuss this matter with Susan; she is aware that I will be contacting you about her grades and absences."*

Don't take it for granted that a teacher, coach, or other leader would understand exactly how such matters should be handled with the child and others involved.

On the happy occasions when you are commending individuals, be specific; make sure they know what they did to get the good rating. Specific comments give readers time to reflect on and "enjoy" the details once again. Consider the "afterglow" following such specific remarks as these:

> *"Your thoughtfulness in remaining out on the curb until I arrived was very much appreciated."*
>
> *"We appreciate the care you take in giving thorough instructions to the students who seem behind in the class."*
>
> *"Thank you for wording your disciplinary action in such a tactful way before the class."*
>
> *"Thank you for the inordinate amount of time such tournaments must require."*

When the situation has become or could become a negative one, use a supportive and firm, but nonconfrontational tone. Commend the organization, if appropriate, for past actions, standards, concerns, and accomplishments.

> *"Thank you for investigating this situation and reporting back to me about the action you've taken."*
>
> *"We hope these suggestions will eliminate the ambiguities in the ways the policies have been enforced."*
>
> *"We're looking forward to a more rewarding semester in the spring."*

"I'm hopeful that this clarifies our position with regard to Susan's absence."

Above all, keep in mind that a careless or carefully chosen word or phrase can drastically affect the treatment your children receive—and the situation in which they thrive or survive. Write with their future welfare in mind.

APPRECIATION

• TO COACH OR GYM INSTRUCTOR •

Dear Coach Hayden:

We want to express our thanks for making our son, Tim Fish, feel a part of the basketball team this year. If you recall, Tim transferred into the district in late October just after you had officially ended tryouts. You agreed to make an exception and let him try out for the team the following week, and fortunately you selected him for the starting lineup. That exception, in itself, could have created jealousies among other students.

We, as well as Tim, feared that might be the case. But as the season began, you planned some very important team-building "bonding" experiences for the boys as you traveled to various tournaments to scout the opposition. Those trips especially gave the team members a chance to get to know Tim quickly one on one off the court. Those opportunities made the transition much easier for him in the new school.

By the way, I might add that his grades have reflected a comfortable adjustment as well.

As you may have guessed, changing schools in the middle of the year is never a good situation for any student, but for an athlete it can be disastrous. Such was not the case for Tim this year, thanks to you. We do appreciate your constant encouragement, your competent coaching, and your efforts to see that the college scouts take a look at your athletes. What more could parents ask?

Sincerely,

• To Teacher •

Dear Ms. Vasquez:

We so much appreciate the special attention you have given to Kevin while he has been hospitalized off and on throughout the year. As you know, such extended absences can play havoc with a child's relationships with other students, and you have been particularly sensitive to making Kevin feel a part of the group when he was able to be in class.

Specifically, I want to thank you for the several occasions when you gave the other children time to make cards and write notes to Kevin. Not only were you teaching your fourth-graders penmanship and writing skills, you were teaching them to care about other people. That, I'm sure, is a direct reflection of your own personal commitment to your students.

And what a wonderful idea to videotape their class parties and special days to send home for Kevin. Although he sometimes watched through tears of disappointment that he could not be part of the festivities, those tapes kept him in touch with his friends during a very difficult time.

I'm sure teachers hear complaints from time to time, but I wanted you to know that we in our household and neighborhood are certainly singing your praises. Thank you so much for your dedication.

Sincerely,

• TO BABY-SITTER •

Dear Jackie:

Just a note to let you know how much we appreciate the care you're providing to Matt and Melinda. When my husband drops by to pick them up each day after work, they jump in the car so full of enthusiasm and so excited to tell him about the day's activities.

Many baby-sitters envision their jobs as simply to meet the physical needs of the kids and ensure the children's safety while under their supervision. You, on the other hand, have shown so many evidences of understanding and providing for the kids' mental growth and emotional development. The "art" projects, the games, the snacks, the story times—all these special activities require supplies and extra time for preparation and cleanup, not to mention patience.

Thanks so much for all your extra efforts with our children. When they're happy, we're happy.

Cordially,

• TO NEIGHBOR FOR WATCHING CHILD •

Brenda,

Thanks so much for watching Maria after school these last few weeks while I conducted my job search. As we discussed, I didn't want to select a day-care center and make permanent arrangements until I knew for sure whether we'd be staying in this neighborhood. Now that I've found a job so close by, I will, of course, enroll Maria in Kindercare down the street.

Your baby-sitting help gave me just the freedom I needed to schedule interviews and do the necessary library research on the companies I wanted to approach for a job. I left home every day with peace of mind in knowing you would keep Maria safe and happy. Please let me know when I can return the favor. I'll be eagerly looking for that opportunity.

With gratefulness,

COMPLAINTS

• TO COACH OR GYM TEACHER •

Dear Ms. Hansen:

We appreciate your physical education goals; you have succeeded in making your students aware of the importance of regular exercise and proper diet to their overall health and appearance. I'm writing, however, to call your attention to a frustration for the girls in Periods 1 to 5: They are having difficulty getting showered and dressed and to their next class before the tardy bell rings.

I can imagine that you have some students who take advantage of every opportunity to "lolligag" between classes, talking to boyfriends in the hall or sharing their weekend adventures with classmates. But for other students who are making an honest effort to get to their classes on time (without receiving penalty points for tardies), they need the full 8 minutes after gym class to dress for their next class. On three recent occasions (January 5, 15, and 18), my daughter, Elissa Terry, says they had less than 3 minutes after the time you dismissed them to make their next class.

On January 18, her science teacher deducted 15 points from her test grade because she arrived to science class 5 minutes late, after being dismissed late from gym class.

Would you please give careful attention to finding a way to complete the class exercises so that the girls are dismissed when the bell rings? I'll appreciate your efforts in alleviating this stressful situation for those girls trying to be prompt students. Thank you.

Sincerely,

• TO TEACHER •

Dear Mr. Frazier:

I want to make you aware of the difficulty my daughter, Trisha Cox, is having finding library resources to complete her research papers for your Period 6 history class. The requirement to have 10 books and 15 articles as sources for the paper demands that students go outside the school library to find other resources, and that has posed an undue hardship on the family because of our work schedule and transportation situation.

I have a suggestion: Would you consider putting some of the more popular resource books and periodicals on reserve in the library so that all students have equal opportunity to use them during their study periods and before and after school hours? For students like Trisha, that is the only time they have available in any library.

I understand that some students may wait until the last minute to try to locate reference materials and then complain that all available books are already checked out of the school library. But with the Period 6 students, that often is the case. By the time this class group meets and receives your assignments, students from other periods have already checked out all available sources in the school library.

Trisha understands you to say that they should be able to use their own home computers for on-line research, but all students, I fear, don't have home computers with Internet access. Trish doesn't. And although Trisha is old enough to drive, she doesn't have her own car. Both her father and I have to make alternative travel plans to allow her use of the car in the evenings. During the weekends, she works at her part-time job.

(Continued)

Trisha and I would very much appreciate your attention to resolve this issue. And thank you for your commitment to preparing your students for college and teaching them to express themselves adequately in writing.

Sincerely,

• TO PRINCIPAL ABOUT TEACHER •

Dear Mr. Bonneville:

I am writing for your intervention in a matter involving my son, Ron Hall, and his English teacher, Cherrie Hazlett. Ron continually brings home excellent English grades, yet he doesn't seem to understand the grammar and writing rules he is supposed to be learning in Ms. Hazlett's class. I'm concerned that her instruction is inadequate and that her review and grading of compositions is cursory.

I'd like to request that Ron be moved into another English class for the remainder of the year. If it is necessary for me to discuss the matter with you in person, please phone me (855-8884) to schedule a meeting time most convenient to our mutual schedules.

Let me explain why I am concerned about the English class: First, the test questions themselves contain misspellings and grammatical errors. (I've attached two such tests with the errors circled.) Second, Ron's compositions contain misspellings and grammatical errors that have gone unnoticed and uncorrected. (I've also enclosed two such essays for which Ron received A's.) I realize that teachers do not routinely mark all errors on a composition, but instead focus on two or three skills or grammatical rules for each effort. But as you'll notice from what I've marked, a ninth-grade student should certainly be made aware of sentence fragments and misspellings in a paper, even if the student is not penalized for those errors.

Thank you for considering this change request for Ron. His writing skills are extremely important to his future, and I want to ensure that he has a master teacher.

Sincerely,

• TO PRINCIPAL ABOUT DISRUPTIVE STUDENT •

Dear Principal Bailey:

The after-school wait for the second bus has become an ordeal for my daughter, Megan Hawkins. Another student, Barry Goldman, who also waits for the second bus to Hogan Town, has repeatedly hit her, teased her, and generally made her life miserable for the past 3 months.

During the last incident, on Monday, November 6, he struck her with a baseball bat, attempting to "bat" her books out of her arms. As a result, she missed her bus trying to collect school papers that went flying across the lawn, and came home with bruises. Although the bruises were not serious enough to seek medical help, this situation needs your immediate attention.

I'm requesting that you observe Barry Goldman's behavior, and if changes don't occur, that he be restricted from riding the same school bus as Megan.

If you asked Barry Goldman whether he intended to assault my daughter, I'm sure he would said no. His antics, according to him, are all in fun. And giving him the benefit of the doubt about the incident with the bat, I know that he didn't intend to strike Megan's shoulders, but only her books. Nevertheless, his attempts to tease have gotten out of hand.

Please let me know what action or precautions you've taken about the situation. Megan wants to "handle" the situation on her own, because she fears being labeled a "tattler." Therefore, I'd ask you not to let her know that I've requested your help to correct this situation. Thank you for your commitment to provide a safe school environment.

Sincerely,

• TO PRINCIPAL PROTESTING UNFAIR DISCIPLINARY ACTION •

Dear Mr. Canary:

My stepson, Frank McQuire, was recently disciplined with in-school suspension from January 6 to 16 for leaving campus without permission on January 3. I think that once you review the details of the situation more carefully, you will agree that this action is unwarranted and unfair.

On behalf of my son, I respectfully request that this decision be reversed immediately. Otherwise, I will be forced to appeal to the school board for a ruling.

Once again, let me explain the situation from our perspective. Your memo to the parents about the new restrictions on leaving campus was dated and sent home with the students on December 18. Your announcement of the change in policy was made to the students over the public address system on December 17 and 18. However, my stepson did not attend school after December 16; we left town early to be with our family in Canada during the holidays. His first day back at school was January 3—the day he left campus for lunch with his brother, who works nearby, as he has done on and off for the past 2 years.

Yes, Frank may have heard other students complain about the rumor of the new campus restrictions before he left town, but he had forgotten about the restrictions during the intervening holidays. We, as parents, never received the notice sent home on December 18 because of our trip to Canada.

We believe the in-school suspension is unduly harsh, particularly in light of the fact that Frank has not had past difficulties in following school rules. I understand your position in wanting all students to know that you intend to enforce the new policy, but

(Continued)

"making an example" of Frank will build more animosity than compliance.

I've written rather than phoned to let you have a few moments to investigate and verify the facts as I have stated them. I can assure you that Frank and I will keep the details of your review of his situation confidential so as not to create any loss of face about a reversal in the situation. Would you please phone me today at my work number (445-4488) to let me know of your decision?

Sincerely,

SCHOOL REGISTRATION

• NOTIFYING SCHOOL OF CHILD'S RIGHTFUL GUARDIANS •

To School Officials:

This letter is to inform you that we, Don and Linda Harris, are the legal guardians of your third-grade student, Michael Pompos, assigned to Mr. Frederick's homeroom class. The custody suit between Michael's estranged father and us has at last been resolved in our favor.

With this letter, we are alerting you to the possibility that his father or another family member may make an effort to contact him during the school day. We ask that you continue to enforce your policy of a child's release only to the legal guardians in all cases.

Thank you for your efforts to enforce these policies, which make the lives of your students safe and less stressful for all concerned.

Sincerely,

• REQUESTING MEETING WITH TEACHER •

Ms. Hampton,

I would like to schedule a meeting with you to discuss Amy Taylor's progress in your class.

I understand from calling the school office that your conference period runs from 3:30 to 4:15. Tuesday or Thursday afternoons will work best for me, but I can arrange to meet you another day of the week if that is necessary. Please leave a message on my home recorder (889-9988) suggesting a convenient meeting time. Thank you.

• REQUESTING INFORMATION ABOUT PRIVATE SCHOOL •

Dear Ms. Shortly:

I'm considering enrolling my children in St. Thomas's for the upcoming fall semester. Mary Catherine will be entering the third grade, and Daniel is in the fifth grade. Having recently moved to the area from Boston, I'm afraid I have very little information about your school, its accreditations, and its academic standing in the community.

Would you please forward to me a packet of information, including tuition costs, required immunizations and other medical records, bus transportation options, accreditations, and extracurricular activities available to students? If you have information about parents' support organizations, that would be helpful as well.

We're looking forward to learning more about your school.

Sincerely,

NOTES OF ABSENCE AND GYM EXCUSES

• EXPLAINING CHILD'S ABSENCE—ILLNESS OR INJURY •

Dear Ms. Geer,

Please excuse Anna's absences on March 2 to 4. She had a bad case of influenza, and her doctor suggested complete bed rest. We'll appreciate your permitting her to complete any assignment she has missed and giving her study time before she has to take any tests over topics discussed during her absence. Thank you.

• EXPLAINING CHILD'S ABSENCE—DEATH IN FAMILY •

Mr. Garcia:

Dana Robinson has been absent for the past 3 days (May 6 to 8) because her grandfather passed away. I ask your understanding and patience in the next few days if she seems distracted and fearful. I'll also appreciate any help you can give her in making up her work. Specifically, she was concerned about her math grades and missing your in-class explanations of the word problems. Thank you for your extra help during this time.

• EXPLAINING CHILD'S ABSENCE—FAMILY BUSINESS •

Dear Ms. Humbolt:

David McAfee, in John Crackin's homeroom, missed school on Friday (September 6) and Monday (September 9) to accompany both my wife and me on out-of-town business.

We respectfully request that you excuse his absence on this occasion. We are very mindful that regular attendance is important to a child's overall school success. But we decided that since we are so close to the beginning of the school year this brief absence would have minimal effect on David's ability to keep up with his class.

My wife had the opportunity to attend a convention in Orlando as part of her work assignment, and we decided to take the entire family along and complete the handling of my father's estate. As executor of his will, I have had many obligations since his recent death and very little time to be out of town to attend to the matter.

We hope you'll agree to excuse our son's absence to accompany us out of town. Thank you for your commitment to academic excellence for all our students.

Sincerely,

• ALERTING GYM TEACHER TO CHILD'S PHYSICAL LIMITATIONS •

Dear Mr. Fulbright:

Jamie Garrett has been assigned to your Period 2 physical education class, and I wanted to let you know of his physical limitations, which may not be obvious from immediate observation. He suffers from chronic asthma and has severe attacks after long periods of physical exertion. However, he hesitates to call attention to that condition for fear of being teased by the other students.

When you observe that he is becoming short of breath, please permit him to stop exercising immediately. His attacks after such exertion have required hospitalization and oxygen tanks on several occasions. (Enclosed is a letter from his physician attesting to this condition and his limitations.)

Thank you for being mindful of Jamie's condition during your PE classes and handling the matter discreetly.

Sincerely,

• EXCUSING CHILD FROM GYM FOR ILLNESS OR INJURY •

Mrs. Wyatt:

Would you please permit Jana Priestly (Period 5) to "sit out" during the dance routines for the rest of this week? She twisted her knee in a ski accident over the weekend and is still having some swelling. The doctor assures us that it's only a pulled muscle that will heal with time and rest. Thank you for your attention to her condition. She enjoys your class very much.

Cordially,

PHYSICIANS AND MEDICAL ISSUES

Sooner or later in the typical family, health care becomes a concern. For ourselves, our children, or elderly relatives, we'll need to handle medical records, offer or request explanations about hospital or physician treatment and billing, or express appreciation or displeasure about medical services received. Despite all the health-care revisions in the past few years in our country, the paperwork has not disappeared.

So when handling medically related correspondence, use a reference line, including the patient's full name and address, and any account or billing number.

Begin by summarizing your commendation, complaint, or request in an opening sentence or two. For example:

"I want to thank you for the excellent emergency room procedures that saved my daughter's life."

"I want to protest the way you handled..."

"I'd like to suggest a change in policy in situations where..."

Then state any follow-up action or response you expect and be specific.

"I expect to see a corrected invoice."

"I'd like to have the nurse instructed to..."

"Would you please detail the necessities of these procedures to me?"

"Will you or will you not contact the insurance company on my behalf?"

Give full details as to admission dates, treatment dates, medication, or fees under discussion. And provide any related insurance information: group or member number, and address and phone numbers for filing claims or verifying coverage or payments (limitations and deductibles). When relevant, state who other than the patient is responsible for the patient's billing. For example, if you are writing about a minor child's care, be sure to include the legal guardian's name and contact information.

In the United States, we are blessed with the best health care in the world. Don't let the associated paperwork details discourage you from expressing appreciation when it is due. Commend those who serve you well.

• AUTHORIZING RELEASE OF RECORDS •

RE: Patient Michael J. Samson, Jr.

Dear Dr. Broadman:

With this letter, as parent and guardian, I'm authorizing your office to release medical records for my minor son, Michael J. Samson, Jr., with regard to his recent back injuries.

Please send those records to the office of Dr. Thomas Winninger, P.O. Box 3889, Atlanta, GA 30339.

My health insurance requires that we have a second opinion before extensive surgery, and Dr. Winninger is providing that opinion. He does not want to order X rays unnecessarily, as long as those your office has completed provide adequate detail to make his recommendations.

Thank you for sending these records promptly.

Sincerely,

• GRANTING TEMPORARY EMERGENCY MEDICAL CARE AUTHORIZATION •

RE: Patient Damon M. Lupos

To Whom It May Concern of the Hospital/Medical Staff:

By this letter, I am authorizing my brother-in-law, Herman Johnson, residing at 489 Wolfroth Lane, Waterloo, IA 50701, to obtain and approve all necessary *emergency* medical care for my father, Damon M. Lupos, while I am out of the country on business next month.

This authorization covers emergency medical care only, between the dates of April 6 and April 16, 19—.

The required, notarized signature is provided below.

Signature _____
               Harold M. Lupos

• REQUESTING MEDICAL EXCUSE OR INFORMATION FOR EMPLOYER •

RE: Patient Martin C. Dominick

Dear Dr. Dominick:

I have been under your care for the past 4 months for ongoing foot problems, and will be returning to work as a deliveryman for Oppenheimer Furniture. I've requested a change in work assignments so that I can minimize time standing on my feet. I've asked that I be given a clerical job in the warehouse rather than continuing my duties of loading and unloading trucks.

I need a letter from you, summarizing the medical problems related to my feet and a statement as to the extent of this disability in performing my current duties, which require that I be on my feet all day. With this letter, I authorize you to release any test results or related documentation to substantiate your medical opinions and recommendations.

Please send your letter directly to my supervisor: Harold J. Jackson, Oppenheimer Furniture, 47889 Overlake, Stanton, OH 44054.

Thank you for supplying this opinion promptly so that I can move ahead with my reassignment of duties. I appreciate your competent professional care in this situation.

Sincerely,

• Disputing Billing Error •

RE: Patient Delores P. Huffmeister
   Case Number 3434387

Dear Hospital Administrator:

On September 30, I reported to your emergency room with a severe nosebleed. Although I went through the admission process, because of the busy nature of the hospital that evening, I received no treatment and finally left on my own accord. Today, however, I received a $120 bill for "treatment."

Please remove this erroneous charge from my account and credit card immediately.

During the time of admission, your admitting clerk did begin the paperwork procedure with me and my husband, collecting my insurance policy number and my credit card, saying she was unsure if she could verify coverage at that hour (1 a.m.).

The staff ushered me into a treatment room to wait "about 15 minutes" to see the doctor. We waited for almost 3 hours with no treatment whatsoever. When we inquired once as to why the delay, we were told that other patients had more urgent need of care and that the doctor would be in "shortly."

Finally, we were able to control the nosebleed ourselves and decided to leave the emergency room to go elsewhere. Neither a nurse nor a doctor ever spoke with us about the condition or treatment, or provided any assistance. I might add that we understand the necessity for treating patients entering the emergency room according to the urgency of their condition. But we do not understand the lack of common courtesy in informing us of what was going on during our long wait.

Then today we received a bill from your hospital for $120 for "services rendered for emergency room care." An attached note stated that should payment not be received from the insurance company within 30 days, your hospital would bill our credit card account.

Having never received any medical diagnosis or treatment on September 30, we do not believe we are responsible for any charges. Consequently, we are instructing our insurance company (by copy of this letter) not to pay any claims you may file on our behalf.

Yours truly,

• REQUESTING SPECIAL PAYMENT SCHEDULE •

RE: Patients Susan Gregory and Tammy Gregory (daughter)

Dear Dr. Tomlinson:

Yes, your dental records are accurate; my unpaid balance has been $1400 for the past 60 days. I do intend to pay the total amount, but I am requesting alternative payment arrangements since losing my job recently. I'd like to pay $50 a month toward the balance until I secure other employment. Enclosed is a check for that amount this month.

We have been very pleased with the dental care you have provided for my daughter and me, and are embarrassed at the economic predicament we find ourselves in. I understand that the dental work we've had done is not an emergency situation, and of course we would not have had the work done had we anticipated the job layoff.

We hope this monthly repayment arrangement will be acceptable to you, and I will let you know as soon as I find other employment and can pay the full amount. Thank you for your understanding in this situation.

Sincerely,

• Expressing Appreciation to Physician or Hospital •

Dear Dr. Koenig and Hospital Staff:

As you may recall, my mother, Allison Jones, recently died while under your care at Carter Hospital. I want to express my heartfelt appreciation for the excellent care and the genuine concern you showed during her extended illness.

In any hospital, one expects competent medical care, clean rooms, nutritious food, and reasonably prompt service. We received all that, but much more. I want to commend you on your rather quick process in admitting patients to the hospital. Your staff had completed all the necessary paperwork from the information provided in earlier phone calls and we waited less than 10 minutes to have my mother in her room. And that response was just a preview of the streamlined processes we experienced throughout my mother's 4-week stay with you.

Not only did we find your response to our calls and questions prompt and receive accurate information about tests results, but your nursing staff went out of its way to elaborate on details of each procedure and test. Harriet Flavor, Stu Rotterdam, and Melinda Hernandez particularly stand out in my mind because of their habit of stopping by my mother's room at the start and end of their work shifts to check on our needs. On three or four occasions, when mother was suffering so badly that I didn't want to leave her side, the nurses brought lunch to me when they returned from their own lunch breaks.

Please commend the nurses that I mentioned above and express the family's appreciation for their dedicated service.

(Continued)

I'm sure that when things do not run so smoothly patients let you know of their bad experiences, so I wanted to take the time to let you know of my complete satisfaction with the service you provide to the community. We will, of course, recommend your hospital to our friends.

Sincerely,

• COMPLAINING ABOUT MEDICAL STAFF OR PROCEDURES •

Dear Dr. Bryant:

I'm writing to make you aware of a routinely frustrating experience in dealing with your nurse, Alice Cornall. Her tone is demanding, her questions during medical intakes are abrupt, and her manner of shouting confidential information down the hallway to other staff members becomes quite embarrassing. Not only has she been overbearing with me, but I've overheard such treatment and comments while she was attending to other patients as well.

On one occasion, a patient that Alice had belittled while still in the waiting room left your office in tears, vowing to go elsewhere for treatment in the future.

Although a talk between you and Alice may improve the abrupt tone and questioning, I ask that you make a more specific procedural change. That is, I suggest the policy that your staff does not discuss a patient's condition in the hallway within the hearing of other patients. Confidentiality is of utmost importance to most people nowadays.

Dr. Bryant, I have appreciated your competent care in the past for my entire family, so I thought you'd want to know of this situation, which may be negatively affecting the reputation of your practice. Please phone me at your convenience (455-9994) to let me know you received this letter.

Sincerely,

• TERMINATING POOR MEDICAL SERVICE •

RE: Patient Donna German

Dear Dr. Denzinsky:

My family and I will not be returning to your office for future medical treatment. Although we have been pleased with your professional competence, the new telephone screening procedures have become a real detriment to your practice and our confidence in receiving acceptable service. Consequently, we are asking that you forward all medical records for the family (Donna German, Sandy German, Susan German) to us at the above address.

On several occasions during the last 6 months we've phoned your office about routine issues: a prescription refill, a request that X rays be sent to another doctor for a second opinion required by our HMO, a question about reaction symptoms to an antibiotic, a request for a prescription for motion-sickness pills for our recent cruise, and finally a call to schedule a routine exam.

In each case, we've been put off, put on hold, or put down. That is, return calls promised by nurses have never materialized. Questions to you have been answered by "Make an appointment." Prescription refill requests receive a "We're working on it" response, yet no follow-up.

I do understand the need for some screening procedures and for help in returning your calls on routine matters. But it has become virtually impossible to receive a response or generate action from your office with a single call within a day's time. We simply do not have time to make the necessary follow-up calls to your office to see a request through to completion.

I'm sorry we will not be able to recommend your services to our friends and family.

Sincerely,

• REQUESTING INFORMATION FROM RESEARCH ORGANIZATIONS •

Dear Director:

I've recently been diagnosed with diabetes and have been referred to your organization for information to help me deal with the condition.

Would you please provide any information you have available on dietary and exercise issues, causes, hereditary concerns, and any preliminary data on ongoing research regarding a cure? In other words, I have all the typical questions anyone might have who has had no previous experience with the disease among family or friends.

Thank you for your continued work on behalf of those stricken with diabetes. I'll appreciate any information you can provide for my own treatment and care.

Sincerely,

SYMPATHY AND CONDOLENCES

People often put off writing sympathy notes until they become embarrassed at not having written. It's not that people are uncaring in such situations; it's more often that they're saddened and unsure about how best to express these deep feelings in the face of sorrow or tragedy. But in just such situations, friends and family have the greatest need to hear from us.

Determine that you will not leave your family and friends bewildered about your lack of concern. Express your regret and sorrow at hearing of the death, illness, accident, divorce, or other misfortune. Begin your letter or note with straightforward comments like these:

"I was so sorry to hear that..."

"I feel overwhelmed that..."

"We were so sad to hear..."

"I'm shocked and saddened by the news that..."

"I want you to know how sorry I feel about..."

"I want to express my sympathy at the loss of your mother."

One of the deepest needs of survivors in times of grief is the opportunity to talk about the loved one or the misfortune. Mention something you remember about the individual or recall something you've heard others say. In the case of other misfortunes, let the reader know you understand the extent of the loss and the painful situation:

"I know you depended so much on your father's advice. He was so knowledgeable about..."

"I know you had wanted a baby for such a long time."

"Sharon was such a devoted wife. I recall fondly the many times she laughed at all those jokes you use at our annual roasts."

"The boys adored their father. Many, many times I've sat and listened to them talk about their camping trips and how their dad always…"

If possible and if you're sincere, offer to help in some specific way. Vague offers ("Call me if you need anything") sound empty and insincere. Can you baby-sit? Are you willing to make a donation or cover some necessary expense? Do you have some extra time to take on some of the family members' responsibilities for a few days or weeks?

In the case of divorce, be sensitive to feelings and circumstances of which you may be unaware. Express your confidence that the individual has made the correct decision and offer your emotional support. Consider the following comments:

"I don't want to add to the problem by prying, so I'll not plan to phone unless you want to talk about it."

"I know you have made the best decision for all involved."

"Sometimes you have to act even when the road ahead doesn't seem totally clear."

"We know you made this decision with much prayer and forethought."

"We will be here to offer our support in the days ahead."

"Our home is open to you. Call on us when you feel like chatting about it. What's a few tears between friends?"

Finally, don't worry about polished wording. In fact, expressing your feelings in your own words, even awkwardly, sounds most sincere. Your comments should sound like your spoken words, as if talking with the reader face to face. And, of course, write the letter yourself on your own stationery or card. This is not a chore to be delegated to someone else. Your letter must come from your heart.

• Death of Child •

Nancy and Frank:

The news of Caroline's accident has shocked and upset us beyond expression. It seems just like yesterday that we all played at the beach together and cooked hamburgers in your backyard. Being so far away from you during this tragedy makes us feel so helpless. We can only imagine how devastated you must feel.

I know the darkest days are before you now as you try to go through the motions of living. Please know that we are as close as your phone. And if you find the need to get away momentarily from the visible reminders, we would love to have you visit us here as long as necessary.

We know that only God can comfort your heart in times like these. You are in our prayers hourly.

Sincerely,

• DEATH OF PARENT •

Madison:

When I phoned the office today, Bob Miller told me that your mother had passed away yesterday after a long illness. Although I know she was elderly, losing a parent never becomes easy. Death always leaves an emptiness and brings solemn reflection on the meaning of life and family.

Many times I've heard you talk fondly of your mother and joke about how she cajoled you into eating healthy and begged you to get more sleep. And from what I know about you, I can imagine that you returned her love and concern openly.

If I can pick up any of the slack at the office while you're away handling your mother's affairs, let me know. I'd be pleased that you considered me friend enough to help you through this tough time. My thoughts are with you.

Sincerely,

• DEATH OF SPOUSE •

Fran,

I want to express my deepest sympathy in the loss of Robert. Marriage being the closest bond people experience on earth, I know you must feel desperately lonely and empty right now.

Even as casual friends, Jerome and I noticed and often remarked how devoted Robert was to you. And your children seemed always to love and respect him for the guidance he gave them through their teen years. You all were very fortunate to have such a loving husband and father to share your lives.

We will be praying that you'll find comfort in knowing that you did all that was possible to make Robert's last few weeks so very meaningful for him. God's peace to you.

Sincerely,

• DEATH OF ANOTHER RELATIVE •

Dear Juan,

I just wanted to write you a brief note to tell you how sorry I was to hear about your brother's accident. No one is ever ready or prepared to accept such tragic news. I've heard you so often tell about your hunting trips and golf outings together and how very much you enjoyed each other's company. Memories of those times, I guess, will be even more precious to you as the years go by.

Please accept my sincere condolences. I am sorry.

In deepest sympathy,

• DEATH OF PET •

Debbie,

No one but another pet owner would understand what you're going through with the loss of Smoky. She was such a strong, loving dog, and I know she gave you hours of pleasure, company, and protection.

I know you must still be upset about someone's leaving the gate open so that she wandered out into the street. So thoughtless.

Well, you can find other protection for yourself and your home, but you can't just replace the pleasure and company Smoky provided quite so easily. Dogs are intelligent creatures, and they can form bonding relationships. I'm sorry for your loss.

Sincerely,

• LOSS OF HOME OR BUSINESS IN DISASTER •

Dear Arthur and Laura,

I'm was horrified to see and hear on the news what the tornadoes did to your hometown. And then when Margaret Echlemann told me about both your house and your place of business being destroyed, I just could not imagine the discouragement and hardship you're experiencing.

Of course, by now, I'm sure you've made emergency arrangements for immediate housing, but surely there must be something we can do to help with the business end. As you may know, my staff specializes in custom software for accounting firms. Would you have use for a consultant on site to get you up and running again? I'd be happy to make one of our senior people available to you at no charge for 3 or 4 days if that would help get you operational quickly. Please call me at (555) 555-5555 to let me know the specifics of your setup, and I'll schedule someone to visit your site.

Of course, I'm sure you're feeling quite a loss on the home front also. And items destroyed with a home can never be replaced. You must feel devastated about that. But then I know you two. You've got a strong faith, a solid determination, and a commitment to your kids to pick up the pieces and move on with life.

Our prayers are with you. And please give me a call about scheduling one of our software engineers.

Sincerely,

• Failure of Business •

Dear Danny:

When I phoned last week, I of course heard your tape that your number is no longer in service. Thinking I'd confused the number some way, I did a little investigating and discovered that your plumbing supply shop had closed its doors for good. Frankly, I was very sorry to hear that.

Although I don't know your specific situation, I am reading more and more articles and hearing frequent TV reports that small-business closings are a phenomenon across the country, thanks to the superstores spreading like wildflowers. Competition is fierce. But whatever your reasons, I know you made the decision with much thought and careful analysis.

Still, there must be some sadness in closing that chapter in your life. But after each ending, there's a new beginning. Another battle to fight and win. Another experience to initiate and grow from. I know with your solid decision-making skills and your willingness to work long hours you've probably already headed down another road. I wish you the best in whatever you undertake next.

Sincerely,

• GET WELL SOON TO CHILD'S TEACHER •

Dear Ms. Wiseman:

Annette tells me that you are going to have extended surgery and will be recuperating for at least the next 2 months. These things never happen at a convenient time, do they?

I just wanted to wish you a speedy recovery and to let you know how much the children—and their parents—will miss you while you're convalescing at home. Particularly, the children have enjoyed your most recent unit on the galaxy. Annette has been unloading facts and "mysteries" on us just about every night at the dinner table. We do so much appreciate your dedication to the children and your commitment to stay up to date in your field. The little extra handouts and current discoveries that you add to the class activities I'm sure are not in the textbook and are the result of many after-school hours spent in preparation. Thank you for that extra effort on the behalf of our children.

We're wishing you a very nice rest and full recovery.

Sincerely,

• TERMINAL ILLNESS—FRIEND OR RELATIVE •

Ronny,

The news about your diagnosis has upset the family and me very much. No one ever expects something like this, and there's simply no way anyone can prepare and brace for such a shock.

I was just writing to let you know how much we care. Every time I've picked up the phone to call you, I've become too emotional to put my feelings into words. Therefore, I decided to write so at least you'd know that it was not lack of concern that prevented my contacting you.

I know you must have heard it all before, but it's still true: Medical miracles happen every day—with new equipment, new treatment, new drugs. We're praying that will be the case in your situation.

We will be thinking of you and will be in touch as you begin your treatment.

Sincerely,

• TERMINAL ILLNESS—ACQUAINTANCE •

Dear Madison:

We were so sad to hear from mutual friends (Tom and Tina Clark) about your illness. I understand that you have been going for testing off and on now for several months. I suppose after such a long ordeal, you're at least somewhat relieved to have some closure on the extensive testing and to know what has been causing the pain.

I wanted you to know that you are in our prayers continually. We've offered your name to our support group, and others too will be remembering you in this way. Only God can provide direction and comfort in times like these.

Please call on us if we can help with some of your responsibilities with the youth group. I know you yourself have served as sponsor to so many events, but we'd be happy to cover some of the upcoming summer outings for you. You can reach us at home (444-4444) or at work (Bill at 333-3333; Mary at 666-6666).

Sincerely,

• To Parents of Someone Getting Divorced •

Dear Alvin and Pat:

Someone mentioned to me that Todd and Trish had recently decided to go their separate ways. I know that must be shattering news to you, because you always spoke so highly of your daughter-in-law and loved her like your own daughter.

Although many people don't realize it, I think divorces are almost as difficult on the parents as on the two involved. There are the future plans unfilled, the relationships with the grandkids to consider, the financial hardships that sometimes arise during the readjustment period—not to mention the loss of a close relationship (Trish in this case) important to you both.

I just wanted you to know that we are thinking of you during this difficult time.

Sincerely,

• TO FRIEND OR RELATIVE GETTING A DIVORCE •

Dear Delores,

Kevin Mercer dropped by my office last week and during the course of our discussion mentioned that you and Tony were getting a divorce. I just wanted to let you know that I'm sorry things didn't work out between you two.

Life certainly takes unexpected turns. And divorce, at least from what other friends have told me, can take the sharpest turns of all. I don't want to pry and don't need any details that you don't feel comfortable sharing. I just want you to know that I'll be thinking about you as you make the adjustment.

I'd like to get together for dinner when I'm in Boston next September. I'll phone as soon as my plans become firm and see if you're available for an evening.

Sincerely,

THANK-YOUS

Gifts, hospitality, help, encouragement, notes written to us—all are occasions for expressing gratitude to our friends and family.

No need to waste time before getting to the point. Your thank-you comments should not sound like an afterthought at the end of a phone conversation or a routine letter. Instead, be direct and purposeful with your comments. Thank the reader immediately for the kindness or gift.

Then elaborate on why the note, occasion, or kindness was particularly meaningful to you. Be as specific as possible. Instead of "You saved me a lot of time," try:

> *"Your help before the party saved me hours—the trip to the party mall, the trip to pick up the extra costumes, your stuffing the mailers."*
>
> *"Your note was particularly special because..."*
>
> *"You made me feel so special in the way that you..."*
>
> *"How could you possibly know that I so much needed to hear from you about this..."*
>
> *"The party was delightful—I was so shocked that you'd taken so much trouble to find out the addresses of all my special friends."*
>
> *"You obviously spent an incredible number of hours and mind-boggling emotional effort on..."*

Don't let clichés roll off your pen; it's not the polished formal statement, but the heartfelt sentiment that makes your note most appreciated.

Be careful to avoid mentioning any negative outcomes or circumstances surrounding the situation. *Not:* "Too bad more people didn't show up to sample your great food." *Not:* "You were thoughtful to try to include everyone—even if things were a little cramped." Those comments, often unintentional, will detract from the overall feeling of satisfaction about the gift or deed.

A thank-you delayed is often a thank-you ignored. By the recipient, that is. Sincere comments suffer from delay. Write your thank-you notes and letters promptly.

• BABY SHOWER GIFT •

Johanna,

The football sweats for Eric are adorable! With that suit and another couple of hundred pounds, he could be a wide receiver for the Detroit Lions! Thanks for taking the time to select such a cute gift. Bill tries to dress him in that outfit every time we leave the house; and of course, I have to remind him that the sweats aren't exactly appropriate attire for a christening and the like.

I'm planning to bring the baby to the office in a few weeks and hope to show him off to you then. Thanks for being so thoughtful.

All our best,

• CHRISTMAS GIFT •

Example 1

Dear Paul,

The fruit tray arrived today and tempted us all to a midafternoon snack. Your selection had so many different little goodies—nuts, candies, cookies—that even our finicky family eaters (I'll not name names here) dove in with delight.

Thank you for thinking of us in such a classy way. Our best to your household for a happy holiday season!

Sincerely,

• CHRISTMAS GIFT •

Example 2

Dear Alicia,

You did it again—you sent the perfect gift! How could you know how much I needed new towels? Everything we have is early marriage, circa 1980. The plum-and-green looks wonderful in both the master and guest baths. But then you know how I hate to save things for "company" use only. Big, beautiful, luxurious towels are a treat a woman needs almost daily, don't you think? Thanks so much. Hope you and the kids had a great holiday yourself.

Love,

• WEDDING GIFT •

Dear Cynthia and Sammy,

I'm thrilled with the crystal rose bowl. It fills the vacant spot on my étagère just perfectly and looks elegant. You're always so observant about gift giving; I assume you've overheard me talking about my collection and wishing for more. Thank you for taking the time to come to the wedding and help us celebrate our special day. We so much appreciate having special friends like you with us.

Sincerely,

• HELP DURING CRISIS •

Dear Kay and Don,

I feel a little overwhelmed and crowded now by all the "new" in my life. New job. New apartment. New neighborhood. But the best "new" is a new perspective. I don't have to tell you how desperate I was feeling, still entangled in my relationship with Marc. When things started to go from bad to worse, I almost felt numb. That is, until you two came on the scene.

I just can't thank you enough for all the time you've spent with me. Calling everyone in your network to help me locate a new job here. Coaching me on the interview. Even neighborhood hunting all weekend. The hours and hours you've spent on my behalf seem like an incredible gift. And an investment—an investment in helping me start a new life.

How can you thank someone for all that? Please know how dear you've both become to me. Your love and concern feel like a warm blanket on those long nights as I adjust to my new life here.

With much love,

• HELP MEETING DEADLINE •

Dear Karen,

Thanks so much for helping me locate a printer to handle such a rush job for the fund-raising gala at the hospital. As you know, printers can be contrary people when it comes to deadlines. Promise them anything and give them what you happen to get done—that's been the credo of the few I've worked with through the years on other projects.

But your solution in going with BFI Printing saved the day. I called Marvin, used your name, and mentioned the previous projects you'd done with him—and he welcomed the business with open arms. I might add that he met our crucial deadline with a top-quality flyer.

Thanks for your time in digging through your basement files until you found his name and number. Thanks to you, another civic project with a happy ending!

With appreciation,

• SYMPATHY OR COMFORTING NOTE •

Example 1

Dear Heather,

Your note came exactly a month after mother's death. It was so comforting to know that you still have me in your thoughts. As you may have guessed, the hardest part of grieving starts after all the flowers have faded and after all the friends and family have gone home. When I came in from work that day to find your letter, it was such a lift. I'm blessed to have such a special friend.

Love,

• SYMPATHY OR COMFORTING NOTE •

Example 2

Dear Brian:

Thank you for your kind expression of sympathy after my son's tragic accident. We can never prepare for the depth of despair that such a sudden death brings, and the connection of our coworkers and friends helps tremendously to ease us back into the mainstream of life—physically, if not yet emotionally. Thank you for your card and concern.

With appreciation,

• ENCOURAGEMENT AND SUPPORT •

Margo,

Just a note to let you know how much I appreciate all the words of encouragement to me during my year as president of the school board. As you well know, it's impossible to keep all the people happy all the time. So I just settled, thanks to your advice, for keeping some of the people happy some of the time.

Seriously, this has been one of the most difficult, although rewarding, years of my life. I can't thank you enough for giving me perspective on the big athlete-expulsion issue we had back in October. And your input about the outdoor sculpture at Lamar Junior High was totally on target; you helped me nip that one in the bud. Those long lunch hours with you helped preserve my sanity. And you do need a modicum of that (sanity) to run a school system these days!

I'm prone to become discouraged when I don't feel as though people understand the bigger issues or appreciate the complexity of a problem. And when I become discouraged, I'm always tempted to hand others the baton and let them lead the parade. You must have intuitively known that; otherwise, how would you have known just when I needed a reassuring comment, card, or smile?

Please know that I owe you a great deal of the credit for what turned out to be a successful term on the board.

Cordially,

• FRIEND'S HONESTY AND ADVICE •

Dear Frank:

The conversation we had last weekend has continued to give me food for thought—in fact, I'm still "chewing" rather hard on your advice. It's not easy to hear the kinds of things you said to me about the way I'm living my life. Make your decision, go for it, and don't look back—that has always been my philosophy in life.

But when you took the time to point out how some of my decisions were affecting Sophie, I had to face my responsibilities there for the first time. You were right. Thanks for being the kind of friend you are—and having the backbone to say some hard things to get my attention.

Max

• Stranger's Honesty •

Dear Mr. Symonds:

I'm still rather astounded to have my billfold back—with all the money and credit cards still inside. Believe me, I never in my wildest dreams expected to have someone ring my doorbell and hand me back that peace of mind I so carelessly lost.

What an incredible thing for you to do! And I'm flabbergasted about not only your honesty, but your willingness to take the time to deliver the billfold to my doorstep rather than simply call me to let me know I could arrange to pick it up.

You are a very special person, Mr. Symonds. If all the kids in the world had you for a role model, we would have no need of prisons.

With great appreciation,

VACATIONS AND TRAVEL ARRANGEMENTS

Alas, even fun and games require paperwork these days. There are maps, reservations, passports, cancellations, and complaints to deal with. But don't let the necessary preparation deter you from traveling in style and with confidence that your correspondence has paved the way for a delightfully uneventful (no surprises) vacation.

Summarize your travel plans in a sentence or two as an opener. (You will be safe to assume that your reader doesn't care about all the background and details spurring you to make the trip. Write only about your arrangements.) Jump right in with these direct openers:

"We plan to travel to your state next month and need..."

"I will be spending 6 weeks in your country..."

"My father will be traveling aboard your ship on August 9 to..."

Request information, reservations, confirmations, changes, or guarantees immediately, without fanfare.

"Would you please send confirmation that..."

"Please provide a confirmation number for our week's accommodations with you."

"What kind of guarantee do you provide in case of inclement weather?"

Repeat for verification purposes all dates, passenger names, group or member numbers, confirmation numbers, or record-locator numbers. And include any written documentation for previous arrangements or payments.

Mention any time frames and deadlines you have for making arrangements and decisions. Otherwise, you may find yourself in the unhappy predicament of having your bags packed with no place to go.

If you are commending a service employee, be specific in your praise. Specific praise sounds more sincere than general comments. Also, elaborate about why you are in a position to recognize excellent service (frequent travel, special needs not routinely met, and so forth). Consider these comments:

> *"I travel frequently overseas and seldom observe agents who are so good at..."*

> *"As a guest-relations supervisor, Mr. Maxwell has an uncanny way of identifying with those of us who are less outgoing and thus avoid the spotlight at such parties. I have been embarrassed on numerous occasions at other resorts. Not so with Mr. Maxwell in charge."*

> *"I spend more than 100 nights each year in hotel chains and, believe me, I know excellent service when I see it."*

You can travel confidently when you have tagged all the bases with your up-front correspondence. Time spent verifying the details before you leave home saves time and frustration on the road.

REQUESTS FOR INFORMATION

• REQUESTING INFORMATION FROM RESORT OR HOTEL •

Dear Resort Representative:

My husband and I and our two children (ages 6 and 14) will be traveling to Corpus Christi the week of July 4 and would like some information about your resort before we make our final plans.

Would you describe your accommodations for our family (we prefer cooking amenities and a two-bedroom condo), availability for the week of July 2 to 9, and costs? Also, please state your policies on cancellations or changes and mention any deposits required. Would you include information on nearby recreational activities and their costs as well?

Please send your information packet to the above address as soon as possible so that we can make our final decisions. We look forward to learning about and possibly vacationing at your resort.

Sincerely,

• REQUESTING STATE ROAD MAP •

Dear Chamber of Commerce Representative:

Would you please send us a road map of Virginia so that we can select the most appropriate routes and activities as we vacation in your state? We'd prefer one that includes all the back roads, as well as enlargements of the metropolitan areas.

Any other information you can provide about lodging, attractions, or leisure activities would be welcome. Because we are in the midst of a move, please send the entire packet to my work address: 1357 Noel Road, Nashville, TN 37234.

Thank you for helping us making our vacation plans.

Sincerely,

• REQUESTING U.S. CUSTOMS INFORMATION ON FOREIGN TRAVEL •

Dear Director of Customs:

I'm planning to travel in Hong Kong, Singapore, and South Africa during the fall and would like copies of any publications or any information relative to customs restrictions for citizens returning to the United States from these locations.

Please send the information to my home address, listed above. Thank you.

Sincerely,

• REQUESTING VISA INFORMATION FROM FOREIGN COUNTRY •

Dear Visa Agent:

I plan to visit Sweden in the summer and need to have a current visa for that visit. I'll be staying in your country with relatives for approximately 6 weeks.

Would you please let me know what documents I must submit to apply for a visa and any other pertinent information such as applicable fees, forms, or restrictions? Will I be able to use the visa immediately, or is there some waiting period after issuance?

I'd welcome any other information you can include about health or medical regulations, customs, taxes, or procedures.

Thank you for your help, and I'll look forward to my stay in your country.

Sincerely,

• **REQUESTING INFORMATION ABOUT FOREIGN COUNTRIES** •

Dear Consul:

I plan to travel to the Far East (Bangkok, Japan, and Okinawa) in November and would like some information about this area.

Specifically, I'd like to know about areas of interest for tourists, any restrictions upon travel within each country, opportunities for temporary work there, and any immunization requirements or health-related restrictions in each country. Please provide any complimentary publications and an order form for any other helpful publications available for a fee.

Thank you for a prompt reply.

Sincerely,

• REQUESTING PASSPORT APPLICATION •

U.S. Passport Office

Please send me an application for a passport. Also please include any other information I'll need to complete the passport application, along with any time lines, restrictions, fee amounts, or required waiting periods.

I plan to travel to the Far East on March 3 and will appreciate your prompt response.

Sincerely,

• Changing Passport Information •

Dear Passport Agent:

I've recently remarried and need to amend my passport. The original passport was issued on March 20, 1996, in the name Megan Meriweather. My current passport number is ABC1234.

Enclosed are my passport, a completed and signed change form, and a certified copy of my marriage certificate. After processing my amended passport, please return the passport and marriage certificate to me at the above address.

Thank you for your help with this change.

Sincerely,

MAKING ARRANGEMENTS

• REQUESTING TRAVEL AGENCY TO CONFIRM TRAVEL PLANS •

Dear Janet:

Thank you for researching the various vacation spots we discussed and putting together what sounds like a wonderful itinerary.

Would you please confirm the exact itinerary (including departure and arrival times), deposits and costs for each part of the vacation (the airfare for four, our resort accommodations, the rental car, and the three day tours we discussed), any regulations or restrictions, and any documentation that we need to travel? Also, please include any fees for changes or cancellations of any part of the plan.

Please send this complete confirmation of our itinerary and costs to me at the above address by April 1 so that we can finalize our plans and vacation schedules at work.

As soon as you provide this confirmation, we'd be happy to send you credit card information for any deposits required.

Sincerely,

• SUPPLYING MEDICAL CLEARANCE •

Example 1

Dear Medical Officer:

My father will be traveling on your cruise line aboard the *Princess,* May 6 to 18, on your trip from Miami to Acapulco. He is confined to a wheelchair and will require a stateroom with wheelchair access, located near the elevators, and with wheelchair ramps to the deck.

He will be traveling with a complete list of medical data and supplies of his necessary medications. Enclosed is a copy of Dr. Michael Truman's statement certifying that he is medically able to travel aboard your ship as required by your guidelines.

If you have other questions about my father's medical condition or precautions, please phone me at (123) 456-7899. Otherwise, he'll be looking forward to a relaxing trip aboard your cruise line. Thank you for your kind attention to the medical details to ensure his safety.

Sincerely,

• SUPPLYING MEDICAL CLEARANCE •

Example 2

Dear Medical Officer:

I will be traveling on May 6 to Buenos Aires by way of your airline. I am confined to a battery-powered wheelchair as a result of the amputation of both legs.

If medical clearance is required by your airline, please send me all appropriate forms at your earliest convenience. Any other information that you can send regarding special assistance in boarding, equipment storage, or security processes will be very helpful to me as I make final plans in the next month.

Thank you for your help.

Sincerely,

• REQUESTING DISCOUNT FOR BEREAVEMENT TRAVEL •

Dear Customer Service Agent:

On September 6, I traveled from Las Vegas to Atlanta on Flight 498 to attend the funeral of my brother (Malcolm Fontaine, Jr.) and returned on Flight 567 on September 8. I understand that you have discount rates for bereavement travel, but neglected to ask for that rate during the emergency situation.

Would you please credit the difference between the fee I paid for the coach ticket ($652) and that discounted rate? My MasterCard account number is 4444-4444-4444, with an expiration date of October 1, 19—.

Copies of my ticket receipt and the obituary notice are enclosed. Thank you for your prompt attention to this refund.

Sincerely,

• GUARANTEEING RESERVATION BY PREPAYMENT •

Dear Resort Owner:

We have reservations with your resort for November 16 to 28 for a one-bedroom suite at a rate of $178 per night. Our confirmation number is 123456789.

Because the weather is so unpredictable at that time of the year, we may arrive later than expected. Therefore, we are providing credit card information so that the room will be guaranteed even if we are detained a day or so. My VISA account number is 4444-9999-8888, with an expiration date of May 19—. The account is in my wife's name: Anita B. Barrett.

Please send us confirmation that you have received this letter and have guaranteed our accommodations by signing below and returning the letter for our files. We're looking forward to our stay with you.

Sincerely,

Requested Accommodations Guaranteed by Credit Card:

Signature _____ Date _____

• CANCELING RESERVATION •

Dear Resort Owner:

We must cancel our reservations with you for the week of February 2 to 8. Our confirmation number is 9999999.

Our change in plans has become necessary because of the unexpected serious illness of one of our children. If you make exceptions to your cancellation policy for such circumstances, we would appreciate your doing so in this case. If you cannot make an exception, you may deduct the $100 nonrefundable deposit on our credit card, with the credit card information we've already provided.

Please verify our cancellation as of this date with your own form or letter, or simply sign below and return this letter for our files.

Sincerely,

Authorization of Cancellation:

Signature _____ Date _____

APPRECIATION AND COMPLAINTS

• EXPRESSING APPRECIATION TO HOTEL •

Dear Manager:

Our family recently stayed in your hotel (May 10 to 14) while my husband attended a convention at the nearby convention center. The service we received from your concierge, Steven McManus, was exceptional.

My child became sick on the second day and Steven quickly arranged for the hotel van to drive us to a local clinic for medical care and then to pick us up at the clinic after we had seen the doctor. That may have been typical procedure; but what follows is very atypical.

The next day when my child had a sudden reaction to the medicine, Steven could not locate the van driver (it seems he was on some errand for another guest). Granted, it was not an emergency situation (just a rash), but Steven quickly volunteered to drive us again to the clinic for another visit. Then he waited with us and drove us to a nearby pharmacy to fill a prescription.

Later that day, he sent a bouquet of balloons and coloring books to the room to entertain my son. And each of the successive mornings, he phoned our room to ask about improvement in my son's condition. His calls showed genuine concern and provided a few minutes of entertainment for my son.

I travel frequently with my husband on business, and believe me, I recognize the difference between service provided because "we must" and that provided from a genuine willingness to help and an attitude of serving the customer—no matter how young that customer may be. I hope you'll share my comments with Steven and reward him accordingly for his service to us. You're lucky to have such a fine young person on your staff.

We'll look forward to staying with you again when our plans call for travel to Baltimore.

Sincerely,

• COMPLAINING TO HOTEL •

Dear Manager:

I stayed in your hotel three nights (January 5 to 7) and experienced a traveler's nightmare during the visit: unsafe conditions, limited service in your restaurant and from the room-service menu, and inadequate maid service. Had I not been unable to find other accommodations on this convention-packed weekend, I would have left your hotel after the first night of inexcusable service. Because of unavailable accommodations elsewhere, I was forced to endure for the duration of the stay.

Considering the circumstances detailed below, I believe I'm justified in requesting at least a 50 percent refund of the final bill (enclosed). The clerk who checked me on the morning of my departure had no authority to make any adjustment and suggested that I write this letter.

First the unsafe conditions: After I unpacked my bags and dressed for bed, another guest mistakenly barged in because he had been given a key to the same room. Upon retiring for the night, I discovered that the adjoining door to the next room was unlocked and broken. Then, after calling for repair, I had to wait 2 hours for someone to come to my room to repair the lock.

The following morning, I waited 50 minutes for room service for breakfast (the order was placed the evening before). The next morning, room service did not deliver my breakfast at all, claiming it never received the order. That evening, I tried to have dinner in your informal restaurant. It was 15 minutes before anyone approached my table to take my order. Then when I did order, the waitress returned to the table twice to tell me that the menu item was not in stock and asked me to make another selection.

As for maid service, I could tell only that my bed had been made and new towels delivered each day. No vacuuming. No bathroom cleanup.

It is clear that your hotel is badly understaffed. Had I chosen a less expensive hotel at cheaper rates, I might have excused such problems. But this type of environment and service is totally out of character for a hotel chain of your fame.

Please let me hear from you immediately about the adjustment to my bill.

Sincerely,

• COMPLAINING TO AIRLINE •

Dear Customer Service Representative:

I'm writing you regarding my dissatisfaction about the way in which your agent handled a situation involving a damaged piece of luggage during my trip from San Francisco to West Palm Beach on April 17, Flight 466.

At the conclusion of the incident, your representative told me to have the damaged bag repaired and enclose the receipt with my claim form and wait for reimbursement. I took the form and left the airport, but upon later reflection I decided that I did not want to handle the incident in that manner. Instead, I want reimbursement for the purchase of a new bag.

When the bag came off the plane, the hinges had become mangled, the sides were crushed, and clothes were hanging out on all sides. To make matters worse, the agent on duty showed no concern about the situation, preferring instead to "process us" quickly so that she could take her lunch break. Because there were seven other people waiting in line with damaged bags, I did not press her quick decision that I should be the one to do the work—take it for repair and fill out a claim form.

However, upon examining the bag more closely, I determined that any repair would be unacceptable with such damage. And because I had immediate need of a bag for a trip 2 days later, I purchased another one. Thus, I'm the enclosing the receipt for that replacement bag rather than an estimate for the damage on my older bag.

Please send my reimbursement check immediately.

Sincerely,

OTHER RESOURCES BY DIANNA BOOHER

BOOKS

Communicate with Confidence: How to Say It Right the First Time and Every Time

The Complete Letterwriter's Almanac

Executive's Portfolio of Model Speeches for All Occasions

Freshcut Flowers for a Friend

Get a Life without Sacrificing Your Career

Great Personal Letters for Busy People

Good Grief, Good Grammar

The New Secretary: How to Handle People as Well as You Handle Paper

To the Letter: A Handbook of Model Letters for the Busy Executive

Send Me a Memo

Winning Sales Letters

Clean Up Your Act

Writing for Technical Professionals

Would You Put That in Writing?

67 Presentation Secrets to Wow Any Audience

VIDEOTAPES

Basic Steps for Better Business Writing (series)
Business Writing: Quick, Clear, Concise
Closing the Gap: Gender Communications Skills
Cutting Paperwork: Management Strategies
Cutting Paperwork: Support Staff Strategies

AUDIOTAPE SERIES

Get Your Book Published
People Power
Write to the Point: Business Communications from Memos to Meetings

SOFTWARE (DISKS AND CD-ROM)

Effective Editing
Effective Writing
Good Grief, Good Grammar
More Good Grief, Good Grammar
Model Business Letters
Model Personal Letters
Model Sales Letters
Model Speeches and Toasts
Ready, Set, NeGOtiate

WORKSHOPS

Customer Service Communications

Developing Winning Proposals

Effective Writing

Good Grief, Good Grammar

Leading and Participating in Productive Meetings

Listening Until You Really Hear

Negotiating So That Everyone Feels Like a Winner

People Power (interpersonal skills)

Presentations That Work

Resolving Conflict without Punching Someone Out

Technical Writing

SPEECHES

Communicating CARE to Customers

Communication: From Boardroom to Bedroom

Communication: The 10 Cs

The Gender Communication Gap: "Did You Hear What I Think I Said?"

Get a Life Without Sacrificing Your Career

The Plan and the Purpose—Despite the Pain and the Pace

Platform Tips for the Presenter

Putting Together the Puzzle of Personal Excellence

Write This Way to Success

You Are Your Future: Employable for a Lifetime

FOR MORE
INFORMATION

Booher Consultants, Inc.

4001 Gateway Dr.

Colleyville, TX 76034-5917

Phone: 817-318-6000

Booher@compuserve.com

Dianna Booher and her staff travel internationally, speaking and presenting seminars and training workshops on communication and motivational topics.

ABOUT THE AUTHOR

Dianna Booher is an internationally recognized business communications expert and the author of 29 books, including *Communicate with Confidence* and *Get a Life Without Sacrificing Your Career*, both published by McGraw-Hill. She is founder and president of Booher Consultants, which has offices in Dallas and Houston. Among her clients are NASA, the Department of the Army, and many Fortune 500 companies, including IBM, Exxon, Mobil Oil, Frito-Lay, US West, Sara Lee, and Pennzoil.